ONE TIME

THE STORY OF A SOUTH

OFFICER

MW00424998

Copyright (1997 by Brian S. Bentley)

ISBN 1-890632-03-1

This book is based on actual events involving the author. The names of some persons, dates and locations have been changed. The author's views and opinions do not necessarily reflect the opinion of the entire Los Angeles Police Department.

This book is dedicated to the memory of Officer Kevin Gaines, who was gunned down while off-duty, by a fellow officer.

Second edition

CONTENTS

ACKNOWLEDGMENTS

I give thanks to God for being my best partner and the ultimate backup. I thank Him for never leaving my side and matching me stride for stride when no other partner could. I thank Him for keeping me alive and sane. I promise I'll be back!

PREFACE

I was not eager to write this book so early in my career. This book was supposed to be written twenty-five years from now, after I had retired from the Los Angeles Police Department. Then, I would have been exempt from the assured persecution that would follow the publication of this book. Unfortunately, just as a dying man's life flashes before him, my life flashes in front of me, as my death is almost certain.

I cannot think of any other profession besides law enforcement that requires its employees to discontinue their relationship with friends and family members who are considered socially undesirable. New recruits are under the false impression that the LAPD will become their new extended family. Unlike a paternal family which sticks by its members during troubled times, the LAPD family can abruptly end at anytime by a single stroke of an unconcerned captain's pen.

My family is not exempt from the social diseases that plague the Black community. Although my closest relative and alter ego is a reputed member of one of the most notorious gangs in Los Angeles, I have not excluded him as my family member.

As I reflect on the events that led to my current situation, I am neither looking for sympathy nor am I making excuses for my actions. These are merely my personal feelings about the pain and anguish I have felt while trying to eliminate others' sorrows.

I apologize to anyone who is offended by the content of this book but life in the ghetto is in itself offensive!

POLICE FORCE

"Horseback-riding trails could be found all over the city, including along the middle of Sunset Boulevard and in Beverly Hills. South Central L.A. was still a pleasant middle-class neighborhood inhabited by many people I knew."

Former LAPD chief Daryl Gates as a rookie officer. ("My life in the LAPD, Chief Daryl F. Gates" July 1992)

After my year of probation, or as television calls it, *the rookie year*, everyone in my academy class was given the opportunity to request three divisions in which they wanted to work. My three choices were all in *da hood*. Almost everyone including officers coming from Iowa and Nebraska chose 77th Division as their first choice because it was rumored to have the most action.

I wondered how someone from Iowa or Nebraska could now anything about *da hood*. As a confused recruit, I also wondered why someone who had rarely seen a Black or Mexican person would want to work in the middle of South Central Los Angeles which was predominately Black and Mexican.

My reasons for wanting to work in *da hood* were so I could help the community in which I lived. As an eager young officer, my mission was solely of peace and good will, not that of a search and destroy mission as so many other officers pledge to do.

I eliminated 77th Division after speaking to several Black officers who had more time on the job than I. According to them, 77th Division was rumored to have the most outwardly racist officers out of all the division in South Central Los

1

Angeles. Allegedly, there were a number of White and Hispanic officers who went out of their way to make Black officers feel uncomfortable. They made rude and insensitive remarks about Black citizens to deter Black officers from transferring to the division. Too many righteous Black officers were a threat to their Wild West culture. There was also a rumor circulating on the streets that large amounts of money and drugs often disappeared after being confiscated by 77th Division officers. I didn't know if these rumors were true or not but it wasn't worth my sanity to take a chance.

Finally, the day came when I had to transfer to another division. I was paroled from the filthy rich area of West Los Angeles Division (the home of O.J. Simpson but that's another story) to Southwest Division on Martin Luther King Blvd. and Denker Ave. It was fitting the police station was located on Martin Luther King Blvd. because majority of the officers in the division were Afro- American. In fact, over half of the officers in the division were Black. That was pretty rare for a police department with over twenty divisions. In some areas of the city a person would be lucky to see one Black officer in a crowded roll call room. To see ten was most unusual.

At the time of my arrival racial tension hovered over the station like a thick dark cloud. Black officers often interrupted the traditional anti-minority rhetoric during roll call by verbally expressing their opposing views to the watch commander. This was probably the only station in the city where this occurred on a regular basis.

Southwest had the second largest population of Black officers next to Wilshire Division which was nicknamed *The plantation*. The Black Wilshire Division officers were

2

comparable to good, happy, house negroes while the Black Southwest officers were like unhappy field negroes. Almost everyone at Southwest was an angry, outspoken rebel. It was only fitting that a social rebel like myself be assigned there. My peers had called me an angry Black man on several occasions.

Unfortunately, at the time of my arrival, the division was recovering from a highly publicized multi-million dollar lawsuit. Several police officers from the division demolished an alleged rock house on 39th St. and Dalton Ave. Patrol officers smashed walls, tore up floors and threw toilets out of windows. It was crazy!

On top of that two officers from the division were in the county jail awaiting trial for robbery and rape charges. The station motto was *We don't get days, we get time*. The motto meant officers didn't get suspended without pay for misconduct, they got sentenced to prison for felony crimes. As a result, the division was nicknamed *South's Worst*.

Despite the bad reputation of the division, I was so happy to be there that nothing about the station bothered me. The station was old, dingy, and not up to modern earthquake standards. The marble floors were badly cracked and stained from urine and other undesirable liquids. Walls that were once white were streaked with brown water stains from leaks in the roof but no one complained. My heart filled with joy knowing I was finally going to get a chance to work in my community.

As I carried my gear through the front door of the station, the first thing I noticed was several big, black and white photos of slain Southwest officers. The photos lined the lobby walls. Underneath each picture was a gold rectangle

3

plate. Each plate stated the name, age, and the number of years each office had served on the job. The most frightening photo was of a young officer who was killed in the line of duty on his first day out of the academy.

Damn! His first day! I thought.

Suddenly it dawned on me, *da hood* was for real. I wasn't in a rap video or a movie where the good guy always won. If something went down, Starsky and Hutch or Reed and Malloy from *Adam 12* weren't going to save me. A cold chill ran through my body as I stood in the lobby looking into the eyes of the young deceased officers. Like the warning on a poison bottle, their eyes were telling me to be careful, *South Central LA is dangerous. It's no joke!*

Not once had I ever feared for my safety since coming on the job. Tactical approaches on traffic stops and on radio calls were just a formality. Now, I felt differently. Taking a deep breath, I prayed to God, *Please don't ever let my picture get hung on that wall.*

After roll call, I went into the report writing room to stock my equipment bag with extra reports. I entered the report writing room and saw two officers booking a shotgun and an AK-47 assault rifle they had recovered from the front seat of a car.

"How did you guys get those?" I asked the officers who were busy writing a property report.

"On a routine traffic stop," one calmly answered.

Looking at the weapons, I asked myself, *Is this what they call a routine traffic stop in* da hood?

What did I get myself into? I asked myself.

4

All of a sudden I wasn't so eager to go out on patrol. For the first time in my life, I was starting to have serious doubts about my abilities as a police officer. In fact I was scared to death. I wondered how I would handle myself in a real life-threatening situation. Who knew maybe my family and friends were right; South Central LA was not for me. My fears were compounded by the fact that my rookie year of patrolling the mild mannered West LA area had only developed my ticket writing skills and distrust for my coworkers.

Panicking, my mind scrambled as I tried to remember the basic fundamentals of computer login, searching procedures, and writing reports. For some strange reason the patrol car seemed like a V6 coffin with lights and sirens. It was awfully damn tight and vulnerable to an ambush.

Should I fasten my seat belt? I wondered. *What if I need to get out of the car quickly to chase someone or to defend myself? A seat belt could mean the difference between life and death.*

The moment my partner put the patrol car in gear, my blood pressure started to rise. I was terrified. I felt like a target. Even though the area was my home, I still didn't feel safe. As a civilian I felt safe as long as I wore the right color clothing and stayed off certain streets. As a cop it was my duty to drive down those forbidden streets.

Southwest Division was like an oasis. One could find beautiful two-story English style homes surrounded by rows of tall, green trees and grass. The residents of these streets could range from a young Black couple to an elderly Asian family. On the very next street, a person could find ten gun toting, drug dealing, forty ounce beer drinking gang

5

members standing in front of a rundown, low income apartment complex.

Like two brave crime fighters ready to save the city, we slowly pulled out of the station parking lot. Directly across the street from the police station was a small group of hard-core crip gang members who were casually congregating in front of a dingy house. It didn't seem right to have the enemy so close to the fort with only a yellow dotted line between us. Each gang member curiously stared into the window of the patrol car as it drove by. From the moment we pulled out of the station, it was clear that the division belonged to the gang members and the police were only there on a work visa.

My partner was a typical thirty year old, tobacco chewing, pickup truck driving, country music listening, cowboy boot wearing good-ole boy, accentuated by him being a former Navy Seal. He was a muscular man of medium height. Impressively, there wasn't a wrinkle in his uniform or a spot of dullness on his boots. Whoever tailored his shirt deliberately tapered the sleeves one size too small so his triceps looked bigger. The *good-ole boy's* sleeves squeezed his arms so tightly I wondered if he had any feeling in his arms.

Holding a wad of tobacco in his right cheek, he said, "If some crap goes down, I like to run after these knuckleheads. How about you?"

Embarrassed, I told my partner I didn't know because I had never been in a foot pursuit before. Coming from West LA had limited my field experience.

"You kidding me man! What the heck did you do to get sent there?" he asked.

6

Three blocks away from the station, the black and white stopped at a red light at Normandie Avenue and Martin Luther King Blvd. I noticed a nicely dressed young Black man standing on the corner bus stop waiting for a bus.

With a bubbly smile, I stuck my head out of the window and sincerely said, "Good evening sir. How are you doing?"

Frowning, the young man reached down and grabbed the crotch of his pants with his left hand. Raising the other hand, he gave me the middle finger and shouted, "Screw you! You Rodney King beating cop! Suck on this!"

"Rodney King beating cop? I wasn't there!" I replied.

"So what! You still a Rodney King beating cop, punk!"

Oh my God! I can't believe he just talked to me like that.

Although I wasn't anywhere near the Rodney King beating, I will never forget where I was when I first saw the videotape. March 3, 1991, I was a rookie officer. I was standing at ease in the watch commander's office waiting for him to approve an arrest report. I noticed the television was on and the watch commander's attention was drawn to the evening news. This was unusual because I had never seen the television on before, not even during the World Series. I turned toward the television and could not believe what I was seeing. Two LAPD officers were badly beating a Black man with batons while he lay on the ground. I remembered friends telling me stories about how the Los Angeles County Sheriffs beat them but I never envisioned anything like what I was seeing on television. All I could think of at the time was, *I'm glad I wasn't there.*

The officers in West LA Division didn't receive much static from citizens regarding the Rodney King incident. At least twice a day, someone would pull up next to my patrol car and say, "Great job! Rodney King got what he deserved. Keep up the good work!" Confused, *I didn't know whether to say thank you or forget you!*

Unlike the divisions located in the minority communities, West LA Division had no one picketing outside of its station nor was there any evidence of low morale among the officers.

SHOCKED BY THE YOUNG MAN'S ANGER, MY HEART SUNK INTO MY STOMACH. I developed a somber look on my face because my feelings were deeply hurt by my Afro-American brother's remarks. I naively thought my Black brother could somehow see the trials and tribulations I had experienced as a police officer, making me different from most police officers. Not so! In the young man's eyes, I was no different than any other man or woman wearing a LAPD uniform. If anything, the young man probably hated me more because I was a Black man in a blue Uncle Tom uniform and working for the White man.

"I hate it when knuckleheads like that blame every cop in South Central LA for what happened in the valley. It's not fair. We shouldn't have to suffer for someone else's actions," my partner said. "I mean. Man! We beat people down here too, but not that long. Those guys just screwed up royally! Do you wanna jack that guy up for bad mouthing you?" (Meaning stop, search and run a person for warrants)

8

I didn't see a need to take the issue any further. "Naw, that's okay. He's just venting his frustrations. That's all."

The midnight sky was indeed beautiful, but contradicting in its violence and beauty. When I first learned I was going to work from 10:00 p.m. until 7:00 a.m., I was disappointed because Black officers quietly referred to the morning watch as the *Klan watch*. This was the only watch where my Black brothers were nonexistent. I was also upset because I figured the streets would be empty. I was wrong! The streets never emptied. Rock cocaine addicted *base heads* slowly paraded in pairs down the main avenues looking for their next high. *Base heads* or cluckers literally walked up and down, back and forth, like zombies from sun-up to sundown. Like rodents, they picked up and carried off anything that was not chained down. They took flowerpots, bicycles, hubcaps you name it. The sight of them was enough to make me sick. I wondered what the lost souls were or could have been if it weren't for their addiction. I was wide-eyed in disbelief as I stared out the car window. Out of disgust I shook my head from side to side.

"That's a damn shame! I don't understand how so many people can be on crack. How did this happen?" I asked my partner.

"Who cares? They all should be lined up and shot. That would save tax payers a lot of money."

"I don't think that's the answer."

"We should nuke the whole God forsaken area! That'll do it!" he came back.

"Something has to be done. This is ridiculous!"

9

FROM PERSONAL EXPERIENCE, I HAD SEEN A NUMBER OF MY OLD HIGH SCHOOL CLASSMATES GO FROM COCAINE DEALERS TO HOMELESS DRUG ADDICTS. For some reason, I thought their situation was unusual and rare. I didn't know the severity of the problem. As I drove from block to block, neighborhood after neighborhood, I saw for myself just how devastating the problem was. The faces on a couple of the addicts looked familiar which caused me to have flash backs to my childhood. I wondered what some of my old friends were up to and if I'd see them on the street. Rumors circulated around my old neighborhood that some of the guys who were on the high school football team were so strung out that they were performing oral sex on men for cocaine. At one point, things got really bad around the old neighborhood. My parents would often be awakened during the middle of the night by one of my old friends ringing the doorbell.

"Excuse me. I'm a friend of your son. My car ran out of gas and I need to borrow twenty-dollars," my old friends would say.

And then there was my cousin Ray. Ray wasn't a drug addict. He was addicted to crime. Ray was a gang member, a Rollin Sixties crip who often lurked around the Southwest area looking for trouble. My cousin Ray and I were practically brought up as twins. Every Sunday morning, my mother would dress us alike and send us off to Sunday school. Every day we would challenge one another by fist fighting and racing down the street. We were the best of friends and fierce competitors. Now that I was a South Central Los Angeles

10

police officer and Ray a South Central LA gang member, we could become enemies.

WE WERE PATROLLING THE AREA OF NORMANDIE AVE. AND ADAMS BLVD. AT THREE IN THE MORNING WHEN I spotted a beat up old station wagon stopped at a red light several blocks ahead. A gut feeling told me something was suspicious about the car. Pointing to the car, I asked my partner who was driving to speed up to it. Launching through red lights and intersections, my partner swooped behind the old station wagon.

Inside were four stiff-necked Mexican gang members referred to as cholos in Spanish. The gang members nervously stared forward as I carefully looked the car over from behind. Suddenly, the driver of the car stepped on the gas pedal. Speeding through the red light, the station wagon fishtailed while the tires screeched and burned rubber. Covering my eyes, I trembled and squirmed as the station wagon narrowly missed hitting three cars as it accelerated through the intersection. Right about this time, I was glad I opted to wear my seat belt. My partner's fast driving caused my breath to shorten. I desperately gasped for air. The patrol car was traveling so fast through the intersection that there was no way he could stop to avoid a collision with crossing traffic. I felt like a human crash test dummy. In the academy, recruit officers were taught that car accidents were the most common cause of on-duty deaths. Right about now, I was afraid my partner would make me a statistic. My partner didn't appear to be concerned as he continued speeding.

"G-ride! G-ride!" he yelled. "Get us a back up and an air unit, quick!" *G-ride* was short for grand theft auto or in layman terms, a stolen car.

Hands nervously shaking, I picked up the mic and took a deep breath. "Three Adam Fifteen, we are following a code thirty-seven vehicle east bound Adams Blvd. approaching Normandie Ave., requesting a backup and an air unit."

Those few words were the most difficult and frightening words I had ever spoken. Most officers, including veterans, got so excited when they were following a stolen car they froze up or screamed into the microphone. In either case, no one could figure out where they were to help him or her. So far, I was proud of my broadcasting.

The station wagon continued accelerating through red lights without hesitation, reaching a top speed of seventy miles per hour. Still traveling at seventy miles per hour, the driver attempted to make a right turn on Juliet St. The driver suddenly lost control of the car and slammed head on into a parked tow truck. The crash looked and sounded like a big explosion. Glass and debris flew high into the air immediately upon impact.

All the air in my lungs froze like ice and my heart stopped functioning for a brief moment. A frightening thought entered my mind as I envisioned the gruesome sight of four dead, mangled and bloody teenage bodies lying decapitated in the station wagon. Time seemed to stand still.

"Damn! They've gotta be dead!" I yelled.

"Oh my God!"

"Shall I request an ambulance?" I asked him.

"Damn!"

12

Seconds later, all four doors on the station wagon simultaneously opened. Before I could blink, four cholos wearing baggy pants bailed out of the station wagon. They held up their pants with one hand and pumped their arms with the other as they ran eastbound through an alley. Every few seconds, one would turn around and see if we were coming after them.

By the time I got out of the patrol car the car thieves were at least fifty yards ahead of me. My arms pumped fiercely and my knees drove into my chest as I humped down the dark, garbage-filled alley after the cholos. The alley was narrow with high concrete walls closing off both sides of it. Large potholes and craters containing water almost caused me to stumble and fall. Fortunately for me, my gun was still holstered. I was able to swing my arms wildly and regain my balance. Thoughts of survival entered my mind as I high stepped through the alleyway.

What if one of them turned around and started shooting at me? What would I do?

The only thing that could have possibly shielded me from gunfire was old, smelly garbage, which wouldn't be of much use. If one of them had decided to turn and shoot, the odds of not getting shot were not in my favor. If I didn't get hit directly, there was a good chance a bullet could carom off a wall and strike me. Each time one would turn around, I'd switch to the opposite side of the alley and run against the wall so they couldn't get a bearing on my position. Focusing on the suspects, I was unaware of what my partner was doing but I assumed he was close behind. After all, he was the one with the experience.

13

LAPD's policy forbids officers to separate during foot pursuits but with each stride, I strained and unintentionally distanced myself from my partner. While training for the Police Olympics, I was timed in 10.6 seconds in the hundred meters. As a retired athlete, I still had some juice left in my legs from my younger days when I was a high school and college sprinter. Coincidentally, the chase was creating the same adrenaline rush I'd experienced when I'd run down my opponents on the anchor leg of the 4x100 and 4x400 meter relays. I was also experiencing some other familiar thoughts.

Should I go all out and try to catch the suspects right away or should I pace myself? Should I wait until they get tired and then make a surge? Will I have enough energy to fight it out once I catch them?

Against my better judgment and athletic training, I let my adrenaline dictate my actions. After three blocks of hard, all out sprinting, I couldn't believe my legs were beginning to feel heavy and weary. With each additional stride, I began to feel the weight of my two guns, bulletproof vest, two pairs of handcuffs, mace, and knife. My department issued metal flashlight and baton would have added some extra weight but during the course of the excitement, I forgot them in the car.

Feeling as though I was running in quicksand, my heart pounded hard my chest hurt. I was so tired that my vision became blurred as I opened my mouth widely and gasped for air. I was supposed to be a conditioned officer but I felt as though I was about to go into full cardiac arrest at any moment. Delirious, I swore I could feel the earth rocking. Next, a bright light flashed in front of my eyes like the eternal guiding light of God calling me home. Then, I heard

14

what I thought was the smooth soothing voice of God speaking to me.

"I've got your back partner. This is Air 70 over the foot pursuit in Southwest Division. I've got an officer in foot pursuit east bound through the alley. Give me a back up."

The rumble and light was not of God. It belonged to the police helicopter or as it was affectionately known as, the *ghetto bird*. In South Central LA, the *ghetto bird* was more commonplace than Mc Donald's restaurants. It was just a part of the community somewhat like a mascot. As a resident of the *hood*, I understood why residents were so angry with the police. It wasn't because of police brutality; no one could get any damn sleep because of the noise created by the ghetto bird hovering. As a citizen, I learned to deal with the noise. Often, I would get rocked to sleep by the helicopter's heavy engine vibrations. As a police officer, I depended on it for back up and guidance. Any modern day police officer would hate to think of what LA would be like without it. Usually, the *ghetto bird* arrived at radio calls before most patrol units.

I was amazed at how quickly it had arrived. I never once saw the air unit during my whole entire year while at West LA Division. Every time an officer would request its presence, the pilot would refuse to come.

THE CHOLOS HID IN THE BACKYARD OF A RESIDENCE when they heard the helicopter coming. My partner and I quickly set up a perimeter around the immediate area and then waited for the K-9 unit to respond for a search.

"Three Adam Fifteen, we need one unit to respond to the corner of Juliet St. and Adams Blvd., one at the dead-end

15

on Juliet, a unit on the corner, one block east of Juliet on Adams and one south of Adams!"

On the street directly behind the house where the cholos hid, two Black men in their late fifties were sitting on the front porch of an old rickety two-story home. Surrounding the men were several old broken television sets, old bicycles, and other inoperative pieces of junk. Drinking gin and playing dominoes, both men smelled of alcohol and together they combined for a grand total of fifteen teeth in their mouths.

My partner stood back and let me handle the situation. I was going to handle it like it was supposed to be handled, Black man to Black man, brother to brother. The White officer's responsibility was to act as a backup if anything went wrong. What could go wrong? These men were my people!

I approached the men with a smile, respect and with deep concern. I politely said, "Excuse me gentlemen, there are possibly four armed and dangerous men hiding in your backyard. The K-9 unit is going to conduct a search in your backyard. For your safety, I'm going to have to ask you to go inside of your house until we are done. Sorry for the inconvenience."

One of the men stood up. "You can kiss me where *da* sun don't shine! I ain't going no damn where, you Uncle Tom, sell out!"

That wasn't what I as a naive officer had expected to hear so I again politely repeated myself. The man's response was similar. A slew of profanities flowed from the irate man's mouth.

16

"Get your butt out my yard! You ain't got no warrant! If you don't leave on your own, I'm gonna throw you off my property! I don't play that!"

My partner, who was standing behind me, stepped forward. Pointing at the men he said, "Listen here you sorry bastards. Take your sorry butts into the house now or I'm going to kick your Black behinds! Do you understand me jerk? Am I making myself clear?"

The men quickly gathered all their belongings. Nodding their heads and smiling, one of the men stammered, "No problem officer. You only gotta be telling us once. We like *da* police. Ya'll doing a fine job. A mighty fine job! I was gonna be a cop once but I got a bad back."

Like children being summoned by their mother, the men ran inside the house. Standing there with my mouth open, crushed, and confused, I angrily shouted, "Ain't that nothing!"

My partner patted me on the back and said, "Don't worry about it. Some of the people down here are so screwed up they would rather get dogged by a White person than get treated with respect by their own. You'll get use to it."

There was no way I could get use seeing a Black person from South Central LA respond to rudeness and physical force instead of polite reasoning. I seriously doubted I'd ever come to accept it as fact either.

Twenty-five minutes later, a K-9 officer and his husky four-legged partner, Justice, arrived. Teaming up with the unit, we slowly and systematically searched every yard on the block. Justice was slow. He took his time and carefully sniffed the ground and bushes for a scent.

17

The search was long and tiring. I had my gun drawn during the entire search. It wasn't long before my arms accompanied my tired and weary legs. At one point I was ready to say, "Forget it! Let um go! I'm tired." Suddenly, Justice's pace quickened. I picked up my tired legs and trailed the dog to a backyard. Growling viciously, Justice lead us to a parked car with a vinyl rain cover concealing it. Lifting up the cover, we found our four grand theft auto suspects lying face down underneath the car. Justice had prevailed!

Drawing down on the boys, my partner screamed, "Let me see some hands!"

"What? We were just lying here kickin it homez."

"The hell you were numb nuts! Get your hands up now!" I told him.

After the search was over and the *cholos* were in custody, my partner complimented me on my keen observation skills.

"That was great. Damn! How did you know the car was stolen?"

I arrogantly pointed to my nose and said, "Instinct baby, instinct. I could smell it. The car smelled stolen."

The truth of it was, I was still in the West LA Division frame of thinking. I wanted my partner to get closer to the car because as a citation minded officer, I thought I saw a cracked tail light. A stolen car was the farthest thing from my mind, but I couldn't tell my partner that. If I had, he would have thought I was a punk.

At the time, I didn't know most major arrest began with something minor like a traffic violation or a warning for loitering. If I was going to survive in the *hood*, I had to lose my

18

tunnel vision because it could get me killed. Expecting the worst may not be positive but it would keep me alive.

I interviewed the arrestees while my partner completed all of the necessary reports and contacted the owner of the car. To my surprise, three of the four gang members were juveniles ranging from fourteen through seventeen years of age. I knew the juveniles would only get a slap on the wrist and probation as a sentence. Fortunately for us, the driver of the stolen car was twenty-one years old and an ex-con on parole, which was good. At least my valiant effort would be rewarded with one suspect being jailed and then sent back to prison on a parole violation at a minimum. On the other hand, the other three kids would be at home in bed before the report would be completed.

All four of the arrestees were members of a local Hispanic gang known as Los Harpes, named after the eagle on the Mexican flag. Talking to Hispanic gang members was a new experience for me. As a teenager, I didn't know any Hispanic gang members but I damn sure knew enough Black gang members. For the most part, I could not see a significant difference in the two gangs besides nationality. Each of the four arrestees was wearing khaki pants four sizes too big. Their pants were so large they had to maneuver their handcuffs from behind their backs to their side so they could hold them up. All of the young men were bald, clean-shaven and well mannered.

Every question was answered with "yes sir or no sir." They all seemed to be humble and mild mannered unlike most of the unruly and hostile Black gang members I had encountered on the job. The young men appeared incapable

19

of committing any of the horrendous crimes their rap sheet said they had. Together, they had over six robbery arrests, two attempted murders, five assault with a deadly weapon charges and a possession of a loaded firearm charge. After interviewing the gang members, I escorted the twenty-one year old driver of the stolen car into the booking cage of the jail.

"I need you to take everything out of your pockets and place them on the counter. Then I need you to take off all your clothes so I can make sure you don't have any weapons or dope on you."

"Yes sir. I know, I've done this before sir."

Leery, I kept a close and watchful eye on him as he began peeling off each layer of clothing. With the removal of his shirt, I noticed a large tattoo stretching across his back. In big bold letters, the tattoo read "LOS HARPES." On both shoulders were names of his mother, children, girlfriend and "Rest in peace Pee-wee".

"Do you have any more tattoos?" I asked.

"Yes sir. I've got one more sir."

"Where is it?"

The gang member lowered his right hand and lifted up his penis. I then observed the name of the young man's gang tattooed along side of his penis.

"Well I'll be damned! Didn't that hurt?" I asked.

"Hell yeah that hurt!"

"Did you numb it or something first?"

"I smoked some weed and drank some tequila but that still   hurt," he told me.

"So you're telling me that you got high and let somebody draw on your thingy?"

20

"No homez!" he shouted.

"How do you know one of your homeboys didn't poke you in your hinny while you were tipsy?"

"You crazy?" the gang member shouted.

"Maybe I'll get me one on mine," I joked.

"What would yours say?"

"I'd want it to say, 'Los Angeles Police Department, Southwest Division LA 90062, 3 Adam 15'," I joked.

"Yeah right. Hey officer, that wasn't me driving. I swear," he confessed.

"Who was it then?"

"I can't say but it wasn't me. Honest it wasn't. I was in the passenger's seat," he told me.

"I saw you and you were driving. It's up to a judge now," I answered.

When booking was completed, I walked into the report writing room where my partner was still busy writing. "Hey partner, the guy we booked as the driver said he wasn't driving. What do you think? Was he really the driver or did we make a mistake?"

"He's a better candidate than all the rest. Who gives a damn! He's on parole and he shouldn't be in a stolen car regardless."

It wasn't that simple to me. On television, police movies made it seem like every arrest was cut and dry. Either he did it or he didn't. You saw it or you didn't. From the passenger's seat, the driver looked like him but at seventy miles an hour who could be sure. It all happened so fast. If he was the driver, I didn't really expect him to admit it but it would have been more comforting if he had.

21

I was so hyped up after work I couldn't sleep. All night, I paced the floor and re-capped the night's excitement in my mind. This was the adrenaline rush I'd been searching for. I was satisfied with the way I handled myself but I determined that if I was going to run after young teenagers, I would have to workout a lot harder.

Six days a week, I ran between three to six miles a day and lifted weights with a vengeance. I also decided to acquire a new tougher South Central look. Using a disposable razor blade, I shaved off my flat top haircut and opted for the meaner and tougher bald look.

I have arrived! I said to myself as I posed like Superman in the mirror.

The night after the arrest, an officer suggested the whole watch go out drinking after work to build camaraderie. Since morning watch consisted of a small number of officers who worked during the most dangerous hours, I thought it would be a good idea to hang out with the fellas for a while. Also, a person's level of promotion in LAPD was largely determined by whom they drank with.

I explained to them I would go with them even though I didn't drink alcohol. I also explained that I wasn't going to buy any rounds of drinks because I didn't contribute to alcoholism. The Southwest morning watch officers ended up going to a little cop bar near Dodger Stadium.

At 7:30 A.M my coworkers began taking shots of tequila. Within an hour the protectors of law and order were so drunk they could barely stand up, nevertheless drive sixty-five miles home. A couple of them were already on probation for drunk driving convictions. One hour of male bonding was enough for me. I walked out of the bar to the yells of "Sissy!" and "Wimp!" The rest of the officers drank until 4:00 p.m. and then slept in their cars until it was time to go back to work at 11:00 p.m.

GUNFIGHTER

"Police officers on the street are scared to death to use any kind of force because they think they're going to be second-guessed."

Former LAPD chief Daryl Gates after the 1992 L.A. riot. ("My life in the LAPD, Chief Daryl F. Gates" July 1992)

The following month, I was assigned to work with a young officer. Every morning at 3:00 a.m., we would park in front of a strip bar located downtown in Central Division. We would then standby and watch strippers walk to their cars after work.

One night after leaving a bar, my partner and I received a radio call of a kidnap in progress on the corner of Mont Clair St. and Twelfth Ave. We were exiting the Santa Monica freeway at Crenshaw Blvd. just as the call came out which put us only three blocks away from the call. My heart beat hard against my vest as I heard the dispatcher say the suspect was armed with a 45- caliber semi automatic handgun.

Against LAPD policy, I unsnapped my holster, removed my gun and placed it on my lap. I believed that sitting inside of a car put me at a disadvantage. In the event the suspect decided to shoot, I wanted to at least be able to get off a shot. It was against LAPD policy but the department wouldn't change its policy until an officer got killed and the department got sued. Death alone was not enough to change LAPD policy.

24

As the patrol car slowly rounded the corner at ten miles per hour, I saw a woman in her early twenties running down the street crying hysterically. A stream of thick, black mascara was pasted to her face. The woman's hair stuck out on its ends as though someone had been tugging on it. The blouse she was wearing had been ripped away and hung off her shoulders like an old washcloth.

To my surprise, the woman didn't acknowledge our presence. Instead, she continued to run in the opposite direction of the patrol car and safety. Within seconds, she had disappeared between some houses.

"What's she trippin on?"

"I don't know?"

After further surveying the street, I noticed a tall, thin, and sinister looking young man in his mid-twenties standing near the corner. The young man was standing ridged. His right hand was concealed inside of his Raiders jacket, a sure sign of guilt. Since whoever called the police said the suspect was armed, my pre-conceived notion was that he was hiding a handgun.

"What's he *trippin* on?"

"Let's find out!"

My partner slammed on the brakes and brought the car to a sliding stop. Instinctively, I popped out of the passenger's seat and took a covering position behind the car door. Pointing my gun at the man, I ordered him not to move.

Ignoring my commands, the man quickly removed his right hand from his jacket pocket and then dropped something on the ground.

CLANK!

25

From my angle of view, I couldn't see what the object was but whatever it was, it made a loud sound when it hit the pavement. It was the kind of sound a gun made when dropped. There was no doubt in my mind the object was indeed a gun. The man's next course of action was to immediately take off in a full sprint down the street and then through a dark alley.

This was the moment that I, as a gung-ho officer, had dreamed of and vigorously trained for since my last foot pursuit. Without delay I gave chase after the suspect through a dark moonlit alley. The suspect's long, lanky strides resembled a gazelle.

Like my last foot pursuit every few feet, the suspect turned and looked back to see if officers were still behind him. As before each time he turned, I moved to the opposite side of the alley so the criminal couldn't get a fix on my location. I also wanted to look back and see if my partner was still behind me but I was afraid to take my eyes off the suspect for a second. There was no telling what the armed kidnapper might do to escape the law.

The pursuit lasted over a half a mile. We went over three six-foot fences, through a vacant lot, and down Adams Blvd. past a large curious crowd at Johnny's Pastrami Stand. By now we were both exhausted. The suspect's long gazelle like strides were now reduced to small, wobbly, rickety steps. His mouth was wide open and his head rocked from side to side. Suddenly, he stopped and fell face down on the ground. Figuring he was trying to play a trick, I drew my gun, held my position, and waited for my partner to catch up.

26

Lying face down, the suspect repeatedly mumbled, "Help me. I'm having a heart attack."

As he gasped for air, I laughed and replied, "This time when you go to prison maybe you should try to do a little step aerobics instead of lifting weights so much. No. I think the next time, you better eat your Wheaties."

"You ain't nothing but a little punk!" he replied.

"Well you're wearing my handcuffs so what does that make you? It makes you my woman don't it!"

"You're weak!" I told him.

Trash talking after an arrest just came natural to me. Capturing the criminal was like slam-dunking in someone's face on a fast break. I felt the need to express myself verbally.

The whole incident only took four minutes but it seemed to have lasted forever. Our back up didn't arrive until three minutes later. Three minutes was too long! It was then I learned I had to depend on myself as a backup.

Like a fisherman, I held up my big catch and I proudly escorted my arrestee past a large crowd of police officers and on-looking citizens. Some mouths hung open in astonishment. A few eyes bulged with confusion and curiosity. Unfortunately, a couple of faces frowned in anger and hatred toward me as a Black police officer.

"How can you arrest another Black man and put him in jail?" a citizen asked me in anger.

"He kidnapped someone," I answered.

"He didn't do anything! You arresting him for nothing!"

"You suppose to be a Black man!" another shouted.

27

"You ain't no Black man. You a sell out! You a Uncle Tom!"

In the academy, cadets were taught to ignore insulting remarks because we were told the comments weren't directed at the officer's personally. Insults were directed toward LAPD and officers should not take the comments personally. I tried to ignore the remarks I was hearing but it didn't work. Their comments were beginning to piss me off. I couldn't understand why someone would put me down for doing what was right and good for the community. The man in my handcuffs was dangerous. I had just cleared the city of a menace to society. No matter what the angry citizens shouted, I was proud of my accomplishment because I did what I thought was correct.

My partner and I slid the kidnapper in the back seat of our patrol car. His six foot six frame and ex-convict arms barely fit in the car as he chose to scrunch down in a fetal position for comfort. The three of us then drove back to the beginning of the pursuit to locate the victim and the gun. The victim was nowhere to be found but lying in the exact spot where I first saw the suspect was a chrome plated 357 revolver.

"That ain't mine! Someone else must have dropped that there!"

"Oh sure!"

"That ain't mine! You can ask my girlfriend. She's the one that ran when you guys showed up. We was having an argument."

"Why did you run?"

28

"I ran cause you was chasing me. Why you chasing me?"

"Cause you ran. Why you run?"

"Cause you chasing me!"

It was obvious our conversation wasn't going anywhere, neither was my arrest. We had no victim and the witness who called refused to talk to the police in fear of retaliation. The only crime we had was an ex-con with a gun, which could send the suspect back to prison, perhaps for life.

Back at the police station and in the booking cage, the suspect towered over me in height and dwarfed me in muscularity. As I looked him over, catching the big guy became more of an accomplishment. Suddenly, I knew how David must have felt when he slayed Goliath. Where I was silently gloating, the arrestee was angry and disappointed at himself for allowing a police officer to catch him.

Looking down on me, he said, "You know what?

"What's that sir?"

"You were lucky. I bet you could never catch me like that again!"

Frowning in disgust, I answered, "Please! I can run you down any and every time I choose!"

"I don't think so!"

"So what happened tonight then?"

"I just got tired. I went to bed late the other night."

"Don't make excuses. I guess next time you'll get a cramp in your leg. You're just slow!"

"Whatever! I'll be out soon. We'll see."

"By the time you get out we'll be in wheel chairs."

"I'll be out in no time. This ain't going no where."

The ex-con was wishful in his thinking. He was on his third strike. Any person with three felony convictions automatically got twenty-five years to life without any questions asked. There was no way he was seeing anyone on the street for a long time, so I thought.

At home, as I attempted to sleep, I repetitiously dreamt of the night's events. Tossing and turning, everything that could have gone wrong did in my dreams. I pointed my gun at the suspect and in slow motion the suspect pulled out his chrome .357 Magnum and placed it against my forehead. When I squeezed the trigger of my gun, nothing happened. When the suspect pulled the trigger of his gun, BANG!

The sound of the gun going off caused me to wake up in a cold sweat. My heart beat so hard that my chest ached. I felt a strange sensation in the middle of my forehead where I dreamt the bullet cracked my skull and entered my brain. It felt real!

What did my dream mean? Did I subconsciously fear death?
During the chase, I was so overwhelmed with determination and excitement that I forgot to be afraid. Everything I had forgotten to do in real life happened in my dream.

A week later, I received a subpoena to testify in court on my arrest. A sure open and shut case I thought. Dressed in an expensive suit and tie, I stepped up on the witness stand, raised my right hand high in the air and swore to tell the whole truth so help me God. While on the stand, I thought of my mother. She would always say, "Tell the truth and shame the Devil." She also would say, "The truth shall set you free!"

30

"Did you see the defendant drop a gun officer?" the defense attorney asked.

"Well, he took his hand out of his pocket..."

"Objection!" the defense attorney shouted. "Answer the question. Did you actually see the defendant drop a gun?"

"I heard a gun being dropped," I answered.

"So did you or didn't you see him with a gun?"

"No sir, I did not see him with a gun."

"Was there any trash or bottles lying around the gun when you found it?"

"I don't know," I answered.

"So it could have been a bottle of beer that he dropped. The defendant ran because he didn't want a ticket for drinking in public," the defense attorney came back.

Since I testified in court that I heard a gun being dropped. The case was dismissed because the judge ruled that someone else could have placed the gun at the location while my partner and I chased the defendant. The defendant was on parole, which meant one word would have made the difference between his freedom and captivity. If I would have testified that I saw the defendant drop the gun, then the he would have been convicted and sent to prison for the rest of his life. In my heart I knew it was the defendant who dropped the gun. I was a heart broken officer. I never thought telling the truth would bother me so much but it did. From that day on every time I testified in court I'd think of that day and it still bothered me. A lot of things about being a police officer slowly started to disturb my mind.

Why in the hell did I become a police officer in the first place? I'd question myself.

31

Thinking back, I could still remember the day I made my dreaded decision. One night while sitting at the dinner table, my father asked me if I had ever considered getting a job working for the city.

"I worked for twenty-five years with the city," my father told me. "Once you get hired, it's hard as hell to get fired from a city job," he said.

The next day, I took off work from my job as an assistant manager of a bank and went down to the City Hall employment office to see what jobs were being offered. Carefully looking through the three-page list of job openings, I was unsatisfied with what I saw. Disgusted, I looked up and saw a poster of a Black man in suit advertising the LAPD.

Now there is something that I can get into, I thought. For five minutes I sat in a deep trance trying to envision myself in a police uniform and riding in a black and white patrol car. I decided to go for it and it was been downhill from there.

A WEEK AFTER THAT MAJOR ARREST my partner and I were coming back from U.S.C. Medical Center for an assault with a deadly weapon investigation. U.S.C. Medical Center was the second worst place a person could be on a Saturday night. The worst place was Martin Luther King Hospital, also known as, *Killer King Hospital*, located in the Watts community. On almost any night, especially on the weekends, a person could expect to experience some horrifying sights in the emergency room. The foul smells of old blood and human waste as well as the constant moans of

32

agony were synonymous with the emergency room. Rows of blood soaked bodies waiting to be treated always lined the hallways. To add misery to an already discomforting environment the nurses were rude and the doctors were snobbish prim adonnas. What made it even scarier was that King Hospital and U.S.C Medical Center had the best trauma centers in the United States. If a doctor treated you, you'd probably survive. The trick was, you had to get treated to survive.

Our victim had been stabbed in the stomach but his wound was not considered life threatening. To complete our report all we needed to do was get the doctor's name and find out if the doctor thought his injuries were serious. This simple task should have only taken ten minutes but somehow we wound up standing around waiting for a doctor to look at the victim for three hours. I was so pissed off that I wanted to run up behind the doctor and kick him in his butt. Fortunately for the doctor, police officers had to be nice to doctors and nurses because we never knew if we might someday end up on their operating table. A police officer would hate to be in need of medical attention and have the doctor ask, "Hey! Aren't you the one that kicked me in the butt that time?"

On the way back to the station, we decided to cruise by Adams Blvd. and West Blvd. to check on a street gang called the West Blvd. crips. The West Blvd. crips were involved in a vicious war with the Black P-Stone bloods. Normally, I preferred not to drive and be the passenger officer so I could get out of the car fast during foot pursuits. On this night, my partner was sleepy from juggling his time between his wife, three children, an off-duty job and his six girlfriends. We had a plan. If something was about to happen, I would wake my partner.

The pitch-black street was empty as it sometimes was at two in the morning. Turning off the headlights, I slowly cruised down 29th St. as my partner slept. I loved to drive with the lights off. I felt the darkness gave us a few more seconds of advantage on a suspect. By the time a suspect focused on the moving car, the Black and White would be right on them. Besides, I had been working nights so long I swore I could actually see better at night than day.

Gradually, my eyes began to focus on two cars parallel parked with their lights off and motors running. One of the cars was a new Nissan Maxima. I observed three neatly dressed Black men with dreadlocks seated inside of the Maxima. Stopping about fifty feet behind them, I saw the men exchange money and what appeared to be drugs through the cars' windows. Judging by the appearance of the occupants in the Maxima, I assumed the occupants were possibly members of the infamous Jamaican posse. Suddenly without warning, the front and back passengers in the Maxima opened fired on the passengers in the other car. Forty rounds later, the Maxima sped off.

Turning on the headlights, I followed the car at about sixty-five miles per hour on a side street. As I continued to follow the car, the passenger in the back seat leaned out the window and pointed a nine-millimeter at us.

Boom! Boom! Boom! Boom! My ears vibrated with each shot. Four bullets ricocheted off the hood of the police car. Still driving at sixty-five miles an hour, I ducked behind the

34

wheel and yelled to my partner, "Put out a help call! Put out a help call! We are being shot at!"

There was no response from my partner. Worried he had been hit by a bullet, I turned and looked at my partner who was lying motionless and slumped over in the front seat.

Panicking, I frantically shook my partner with vigor and asked, "Partner, are you alright? Are you alright?"
My partner angrily slapped my hand away and said, "Mommy, leave me alone! I'm asleep."

Astonished, I couldn't believe my partner was not only sleeping but also dreaming in the middle of a high-speed pursuit with bullets whizzing by us.

"Wake up, Wake up, they are shooting at us!"

Yawning, he lazily asked, "Can't we let them go? I'm sleepy."

Boom! Boom! Shots continued to ring out from the Jamaicans' car. My partner wiped his eyes and calmly began broadcasting our event over the radio. Through a hail of gunfire, lights and siren wailing, we continued to chase the suspects down residential streets exceeding speeds of eighty-five miles per hour. The driver never once braked or slowed down before he rocketed through intersections. Fortunately, there weren't many people on the street, although we did encounter a near collision while crossing Jefferson Blvd.

"Damn! This is just like TV!" I yelled to my yawning partner.

Four minutes had elapsed. Our closest back up was five minutes away and the air unit was grounded due to bad weather. We were alone! The Jamaicans lead us into a housing area known as *The Jungle*. Turning down a narrow

35

alley and slowing down, it was obvious our pursuit was about to reach its climax.

We quickly and carefully devised a plan. We deducted that since the suspect in the back seat had already shot at us at least thirty-five times, it was safe to say when the car stopped he was going to come out shooting. Our plan was simple. As soon as the car stopped, we were going to shoot, reload and shoot again until our guns were empty.

Slowing down to about ten miles per hour, the driver and the front passenger dove out of the car while it was still moving. Both quickly rolled over onto their feet and ran between the houses so fast I couldn't describe what they were wearing. The Maxima, with the shooter still inside, continued to roll until it crashed into the back of a parked car. As expected, the shooter stepped out of the car with a gun in his hand. My eyes intensely channeled down between the sights of my gun onto the shooter's chest. I felt my index finger slowly squeeze the trigger. I was so focused I could hear myself breathe. Faintly, as if I were dreaming, I heard my partner repeatedly yell for the shooter to drop his gun.

What is he doing that for? That wasn't part of the plan.

Just as I was about to finish the trigger pull, the shooter dropped his gun and put his hands up. A fraction of a second later and I would have been a hero or maybe even a legend, indoctrinated into the elite status as "a real south end gunfighter." Whenever a police officer killed someone, it put him or her into the elite category of a gunfighter. I was almost there. I could have been there and justifiably so. This was the opportunity almost every police officer dreamed of and I let it slip by.

36

Unexpectedly, the suspect slowly walked toward my partner with his hands up. Suddenly, he growled loudly and ran toward him. My partner had never been faced with this situation during his academy training nor in his field experience, and he froze.

The suspect tackled him and pinned my partner against the hood of the patrol car. My partner squirmed, twisted and wiggled as he desperately tried to free himself from the suspect's grasp. I quickly ran around the car to his assistance. I was in a dilemma. I couldn't shoot the suspect without injuring my partner. I couldn't put my gun away and wrestle with the suspect because he might pull out a second gun or a knife and kill us both.

With my left hand, I grabbed him by his dreadlocks and pulled his head away from my partner. I then raised my gun up and hit the raging suspect in the face as hard as I could. A six-inch gash instantly opened across his face. Blood squirted in the air like juice from a sliced orange. Still growling, the suspect refused to release his grip from around the officer's throat. This time, I struck him over and over again until he gradually fell into a hopeless state of insensibility.

As he finally released the grip on my partner's throat, coagulated blood seeped between the cracks in his head. I was amazed at how bright the blood was. Through the dimness of the alley it almost seemed to glow a bright burgundy color. Slowly, he collapsed to the ground and lay still as if dead.

"Oh my God! You've killed him!" my partner said.

I holstered my gun and attempted to handcuff the suspect. As soon as he heard the holster snap, the dazed and

37

bloody suspect jumped up and ran down the alley. Quickly catching up to him, I shoved him forward. My push caused him to stumble and fall face down on his already bloody face. Reaching up, the suspect grabbed my leg and tried to pull me down to the ground. I was amazed at how much strength the villain still had. Raising my foot, I stomped him once in the head.

"That's for running the red light on La Brea Ave. and Rodeo Rd." I yelled.

While lying face down, the suspect raised his right hand and said, "Okay, I give up!"

Wait a minute! I thought. *This situation looks familiar.*

Learning from LAPD history, I refrained from giving the downed suspect another stomp. I whipped out my handcuffs, put my knee in the suspect's back and cuffed him.

The greatest prize I've ever received was winning my life back from someone who had tried to take it away from me. I wondered why beating my assailant half to death was so enjoyable? It was as if I had done it before. The incident caused me to quickly reflect on my childhood.

Ironically, as a child, my gang-banging cousin Ray and I played cops and robbers every day. I always wanted to be the cop, emulating my idol Linc from the television series Mod Squad. At the end of every episode, Linc would either chase down a speeding car on foot or he would dive over some bushes onto a fleeing criminal's back. I had no idea what the rest of the show was about.

Pointing my imaginary gun at Ray, I would tell him to freeze. Then, the chase would be on. I would chase him through backyards, over fences and down the street. The pursuit would always end with me tackling my cousin. That would lead to a big, not so playful fistfight to the death. Taking turns punching each other in the nose and kneeing one another in the groin, we would fight until we collapsed with exhaustion. Finally, because the good guy always won, I would lock him up in my imaginary jail. Thirty seconds later, his time would be served. Ray would be free to terrorize the world once again. I never thought twenty years later, Ray and I would play the same game but for higher stakes, our lives. No one could have ever actually thought I would one day become a cop and Ray an incarcerated robber.

My childhood game was my first mental preparation in dealing with the inept judicial system. As a police officer, I risked my life and limbs chasing dangerous criminals only to see them get released in little or no time. Looking back, this was probably the best patrol training I had ever experienced. It was far more beneficial than any training I received in the LAPD academy. Without a doubt I had the will to survive! I didn't learn how to whip the Jamaican in the Los Angeles Police academy. I learned how to do it while growing up.

New recruits were under the illusion that shiny shoes would keep them alive on the violent streets of Los Angeles. My Academy instructor would say, "If you keep your shoes and badge shinned, criminals will think you are squared away and won't try anything." My partner's shoes were shiny but our suspect didn't notice or care, however he certainly noticed my dull boots as I stomped him. It's a good thing they where dull. I wouldn't have been able to deny my actions if I'd left shoe polish on his face.

Academy instructors also spent countless hours unsuccessfully trying to teach my recruit classmates how to survive during physical confrontations. I witnessed a third of my recruit class stop fighting and give up after getting punched once during boxing training.

A SMALL CROWD OF ABOUT TWENTY PEOPLE HAD INTENSELY WATCHED a Black officer pistol whip an unarmed Black man in a dark alley. I should have been thrilled to survive my ordeal but in the midst of the Rodney King beating case, I was more terrified after the incident than during. The last thing I wanted to do was cause another riot. I had worked through one and it wasn't very fun.

I worried about what the witnesses would say when interviewed by a sergeant or worse, a news reporter. Surprisingly, no one protested my actions, not even the battered suspect. In fact, a couple of on looking blood gang members privately told me they wished I had killed the Jamaican drug dealer because Jamaicans disrespected the neighborhood gangsters.

While another unit transported the arrestee to the station, my partner and I wrapped up at the crime scene. We looked inside of the Maxima and found two other nine-millimeter handguns and two hundred rounds of ammunition on the back seat. On 29th St., we found an abandoned bullet riddled car left in the roadway. Even though all of the hospitals in the LA county where alerted, no one ever showed up at a hospital with gunshot wounds nor did anyone come to the police station to make a crime report.

Now that the fun and courageous part was over, we headed back to the station to do the paper work. On the way back my partner complained that he was not going to be able to make it to his off-duty job because we were going to be bogged down in paper work.

"I told you that we should have let them go. Now I won't get a chance to work off-duty today. That means I can't go out drinking this week."

In a zoo like atmosphere a small group of about five officers stood in the hallway of the station. Like a rare captured animals on the verge of extinction, they curiously looked into the glass holding tank where the arrestee was caged. Each officer angrily took turns pointing and making threatening comments to him.

One older officer sincerely yelled, "If you would have done this in my day, you would not have lived. If you had lived, you wouldn't have lived long enough to make it to court because that cell wouldn't be safe!"

Another said, "If I was there, you would be dead. I would have shot you after you dropped the gun."

Wading through the crowd, I made my way into the holding tank to interview my arrestee. My breath was taken by his appearance. His face was so swollen and grossly distorted that I had to forcibly hold in my vomit. Both of the Jamaican's eyes were closed from swelling. Several large knots protruded from his head. His face made Rodney King's look like Billy Dee Williams. There was no doubt he would have to be booked in the jail ward located on the 13th floor of U.S.C. County Hospital, a police officer's second fantasy. The legendary 13th floor of U.S.C. County Hospital was a jail ward

41

for inmates with serious medical problems and who needed to be near an emergency center if complications arose. If a person got booked there then they were in bad shape.

"If you can't kill um, beat um bad enough to be booked on the 13th floor." A training officer once told me.

I was now more afraid than ever. I was afraid if the media found out, I would get indicted like the officers who beat Rodney King.

Forget that! They would have to find me first. I ain't going to prison for nobody!

Before I could ask my arrestee a question, he spoke to me with a heavy Jamaican accent.

"No *ting* personal against you Black mon. I just tryin to get away. I want to *tank* you fo not making me dead. If it be one of them crackers out there, I be dead now. I know you kicked my rear end good but you just doing your job, Black mon. I respect you fo dat Black mon."

"Tell me something. How come you dropped your gun instead of shooting at us?"

The Jamaican looked at me as if I was stupid and then asked, "Why you tink? Cause I didn't want to die."

"Do you know how close you came to dying tonight? I was actually squeezing the trigger when you dropped the gun." Shaking my head in disbelief, I continued. "My mind was set on killing you but for some unknown reason I was able to stop. That was weird. Another fraction of a second and you would have been dead. I don't know why I didn't finish."

"You didn't shoot me cause you a good Black *mon* that's why."

His words were meaningless. Judging by his four previous assaults with a deadly weapon arrests, I as a Black Mon police officer, knew the Jamaican didn't respect anyone. I figured he didn't want me to leave his side because he was afraid the White officers would hang him in his cell. Out on the street he was hostile and presented himself in a cold and unnerving manner. Now he seemed nervous and afraid by the lynch mob atmosphere directed toward him.

My attention was more focused on explaining my use of force. I was afraid that if I said the wrong thing I could wind up on trial in some court. After completing the interview with the arrestee, I stood in the hallway and entertained questions from awaiting officers.

"So why didn't you shoot him when you had the chance?"

"Because I didn't feel like my life was in immediate danger," I answered.

"So what. You could have justified it, that's all that matters!" Another said.

"He would have shot you if he had the chance. Besides, if you had killed him, the homicide detectives would be taking the report instead of you. You would be at home right now drinking a beer." Someone said.

"Dead men don't complain!"

Trying to defend myself, I said, "The manual says we are only suppose to shoot as a last resort. I had other options so I used them."

In unison, everyone yelled, "Screw the LAPD manual!"

"So when did you start abiding by the manual?" I was asked.

Agitated by their questions and comments, I responded, "Look, I didn't come on this job to shoot people."

Someone interrupted me by shouting, "I did!"

"If I wanted to beat up and shoot people, I would have become a drug dealing gang banger."

"Aren't you one now?" Someone smartly asked.

"I'm not listening to you guys! All of you guys are saying what you would have done. All of you probably would have pissed in your pants!"

"If one of us White guys would have beat him the way you did, the people in that neighborhood would be rioting right now. Because you're Black, you can get away with it." Someone said.

"The difference is, I only hit him six times. You guys would have hit him fifty-six times." I responded.

"It's better for us White guys to just go ahead and shoot knuckleheads so they won't make up stuff and try to sue us. If the officers in Foothill Division had shot Rodney King then all this mess wouldn't be happening now. He should have been dead before the camera started rolling."

Walking into the report writing room, I asked my partner why he didn't shoot.

"I was waiting for you to shoot first," he answered.

Somehow, I knew he was going to say that. It took hours for us to complete all the reports and book all the evidence. The whole ordeal took over six hours. My partner and I were so tired that we didn't know if we were coming or going. Despite the long night, my partner still managed to work off-duty while I went home and tried to sleep.

44

At home, despite the long night, I was unable to sleep. I was feeling restless and antsy as I reflected on my experience. The night's action was not what I had expected to encounter in my homeland. When I first came to the division, I wasn't looking to use violence or come off as rude. Somehow, the hostile and violent environment started to take over the goodness in me. I felt as though I was being possessed! My soul was being torn in half. I felt badly about what I had done; not because I fought to survive but because I enjoyed beating my attacker.

What is going on inside me?

I was confused and needed a second opinion. Picking up the phone, I called my old college buddy, Lowe, who grew up in the Watts community.

"What's up man!"? (Pronounced main) You'll never guess what happened to me last night."

"What? You met a freak."

"Naw, we rolled up on a drug deal gone bad. These fools started shooting at us."

I then proceeded to explain the car chase and how it terminated.

"I can't believe I didn't shoot that dude. That is freaking me out. I also feel kind of bad that I had to beat this fool down like that."

Lowe angrily responded, "You shouldn't feel bad. He got what he deserved. You were only doing what you had to do. I couldn't be a cop because I'd be *beaten-down* people everyday. You guys go through too much stuff."

"Yeah, I guess you're right. Okay, I'll talk to you later... peace," I concluded.

Laughing Lowe replied, "Yo, peace, you Rodney King beating cop!"

"Aw, that's cold. Why you gotta go there?" I said.

"I'm just kidding. Later."

As I look back, I'd have to say the first hit delivered to the Jamaican's head was as addictive as a cocaine addicts' first hit of a cocaine pipe. It felt so good that I wanted more. A part of me couldn't wait to do it again. I was deeply concerned about my feelings because I knew violence could be habit forming. I thought of my mother's plea for me not to become a violent cop and my family's prediction I'd have to beat people in order to survive.

I was so naive! For some reason, I actually thought I would be different from the many other officers on the job before me. Two years prior, I had told a close relative about my desire to work in South Central Los Angeles. He strongly opposed it because in his opinion the ghetto brought out the worst in people.

"You're going to get over there and start beating up on people like all the other cops."

"Naw, not me!"

"You're going to have to in order to survive. Fools out there are crazy!" he said.

"You're wrong!" I strongly argued. "You don't have to yell at people to get them to listen to you. I'm going to use kindness and sensitivity to make my arrest. I'm not going to hit people or grab on them."

"Boy, I wish some cop would try to use some kindness and sensitivity to arrest me. He'd be in for a big surprise." My relative answered.

46

Even before that, my own dear sweet mother raised her objections about me becoming a police officer. When I got home from job hunting, my parents were sitting at the kitchen table eating dinner.

"Guess what? I applied for a job with the city like daddy told me," I said.

"Doing what?" my mother asked.

Clearing my throat, I said, "Police Officer."

My mother jumped out of her chair and angrily shouted, "Why in the hell do you want to be a low down, dirty police officer for? All they do is beat up on innocent people!"

Looking at my father who was intensely gnawing on a beef neck bone, my mother asked, "Aren't you going to say something?"

Pausing from his neck bone, my father calmly said, "It's a job ain't it? He's going to get paid, right? That's all that matters. Now he can help out more on the utilities. I'm tired of paying all the bills!"

For hours, my mother followed me around the house fussing, cursing and telling me I was making a big mistake. Desperately in need of moral support, I walked around the corner to my friend Terry Jr's house. Terry Jr's father was a Los Angeles Police officer with the nickname of Dirty Terry because he reminded everyone of a Black Dirty Harry. I knew Dirty Terry would be happy to know I was following in his footsteps.

Dirty Terry was tall, lean and mean. The children in the neighborhood gave him the nickname because he not only resembled a Black Dirty Harry but because he always carried a big gun. Like Clint Eastwood in the Dirty Harry movies, Dirty

47

Terry often threatened to use it on just about anyone. Once while coaching his son's little league baseball team, he lifted up his shirt and showed the umpire a .38 caliber revolver holstered in his waistband.

"If you make another bad call like that against my team, I promise you it will be your last call!" The umpire, only eighteen years old, was terrified. For the rest of the season, every questionable call went to his team.

Perhaps he will even take me under his wing and teach me a few of his tricks. I thought as I walked.

As usual, Dirty Terry was sitting in his den watching *Chips* reruns on videotape. I told Dirty Terry I was going to take the LAPD exam on Saturday and wanted his advice on what to do.

"My advice to you is, forget it! Becoming a police officer is not worth all the money in the world. No amount of money is worth putting your life on the line every night. The abuse you are going to get from citizens and the administration will make you bitter. The Department is run by idiots from the Chief on down. Do yourself a favor and keep your job. You will be sorry if you don't."

Dirty Terry's words of wisdom went in one ear and out the other. I figured he didn't want me to become a police officer because he was afraid that one day I would become his boss. Against everyone's wishes, I proceeded with my quest.

SUMMER MADNESS

"How do you intellectualize when you punch the hell out of a Black person? He either deserves it or he doesn't."

Former LAPD Detective Mark Fuhrman. (Based on transcripts used by the O.J Simpson defense lawyers)

I was starting to regret my decision to disregard everyone's plea. In the days to follow, my thirst for violence would become so bad that every night before going to work, I would first pray for my partner's and my safety. Secondly, I'd pray to God and ask him not to let me kill or seriously hurt anyone regardless of how good it felt. I didn't want to become a monster.

Summer had arrived. Southwest citizens were full of anger and malt liquor. Traditionally, the summer heat caused dramatic increases in crime and violence. Now, things were supposed to be different. After the LA riot in 1992 gangs in Watts vowed to stop killing one another and declared a truce. However, the west side gangs made no such promise.

In the days following the riot, LAPD allowed officers to work over-time, which put more officers on the street. In time the over-time budget depleted and things went back to normal. As soon as LAPD decreased its number of patrol cars back down to regular deployment numbers, it was business as usual. While the media glamorized the truce in Watts, the west side gangs began killing each other at an alarming rate. It was almost as if they were trying to make up for lost time. People continued to die as a gang truce on the west side of town became no more than wishful thinking.

The media and the city of Los Angeles wishfully wanted to believe a three-day riot would end a twenty-year war and unify thousands of dysfunctional gang members. Even if the truce did exist, no one promised to stop car-jacking people or give up committing other crimes. What did people expect? Did they think gang members were going to give up gang banging and go work for IBM?

In my heart, I had hoped a truce did exist and would last forever. I knew that even if one had materialized after the riot, some young up-and-coming gang member would break it. The whole foundation of gang banging was to defy authority and rules and to gain self-esteem by causing fear and death to others. I knew this from personal experience. I grew up with crip gang members. I saw my cousin Ray display an unforgivable amount of hatred toward blood gang members. Blood gang members traditionally wore red clothing. On more than one occasion, I saw Ray forcefully remove red clothing from a person and burn it in anger. Ray would feel good after his accomplishment.

In terms of self-esteem, for some, driving down the street and shooting a rival gang member was equivalent to scoring the winning touchdown in a homecoming football game. Getting caught and convicted of murder was like receiving a varsity letter in two sports. If the case got media attention then that person had reached All-American status. A gang member arrested for murder could proudly walk into his cell with his head held high.

"What you in fo?" one might ask.

"187 fool!" The murderer could proudly answer. 187 is the penal code section for murder. It is also a popular term used among rappers and youths in Los Angeles. The seriousness of the term has been lost. Very few young people equate the term with the loss of a life nor do they envision a mother crying over a casket.

There was no simple solution to gang banging. It seemed like almost everyone was carrying a gun. My partner and I averaged three arrests a week involving concealed weapons. Sometimes we'd go a week without arresting someone with a concealed weapon but the next week we might recover four guns during one arrest. Ninety-five percent of the guns we recovered were taken during the riot.

Hostility from angry citizens and heavy criticism by the media caused many officers to go on sabbatical. Even though morale was low, I was compelled to keep working hard. I felt like every robber I let get away was still out on the street to rob me off-duty. Every burglar I failed to apprehend was still lurking about and could break into my house.

Although my efforts to serve the community were noble, I'd have to admit the summertime was not the right time for nobility. No matter how minor the arrest, almost everyone I arrested went down swinging. Their motto was "I'm not going out like Rodney King." Gang members were literally pushing officers around and trying to provoke a physical confrontation so their buddies could capture it on videotape. Some officers chose to turn the other cheek and walk away. Others refused to respond to any disturbing the peace calls where gang members were involved. The officers knew the gang members would refuse to cooperate and then turn a verbal confrontation into a physical altercation.

As a headstrong officer, my ego was too big to just walk away. Besides, I had been pushed around by gang members all of my life. It was now time to stand up and fight. It seemed like almost every night I was grabbing, slamming or punching someone. I filled out so many use of force reports the captain called me into his office and counseled me about them.

"You are doing an excellent job out there and I don't want to tell you to stop arresting people but the City Council and the Police Commission don't look at how many losers you put away or how dangerous they are. The only thing they look at now is how many times you use force in your arrest. If you want to promote, you have to stop using force and in these times that means stop arresting people." The Captain said.

It was around this time a friend of mine who attended Howard University phoned me.

"How are you different from a racist, White police officer who beats up on Black people?" he asked.

"I don't beat people out of anger or hatred. For me, it's like when a father tells his son, 'I hate to do this but it's for your own good. This is going to hurt me more than it hurts you.' The father then proceeds to beat the hell out of his child, hoping something good will come out of it," I replied.

I then went on to explain that some White officers work in Black communities because they despise Black people. They take out their hatred on gang members because it's socially acceptable. On the other hand, many Black police officers choose to work in South Central LA because they say

52

they love the community. The underlying reason is they hate Black gang members and criminals more than they love hard working citizens. Regardless of the reasons why each one works in the community, the result is the same; an LAPD beating!

"Perhaps there is no difference," we concluded.

"How can you consider yourself a role model and you enjoy beating up on people?" I was asked.

"I do it out of self defense."

"Yeah but you enjoy it. How can you consider yourself a role model?"

For many people in my community I could never be a role model. To them I was the enemy, an outsider, someone who was trying to take their freedom away from them. Very few saw me as a Black man trying to lend a helping hand. I remembered the day I promised my mother I would not become part of the police brutality problem that already plagued the community. I was wrong!

My partner during this time was six foot three, two hundred thirty-five pounds with freckles. His hobbies were Chinese kickboxing and collecting automatic weapons. The first time we met, it took me all of three minutes to realize my partner was both friendly and demented.

"Hey partner, I didn't get much sleep today. Let's kill someone so we can get off early," he said.

"Anyone in particular or the first person we see?" I asked.

"How about this? Let's shoot an old handicapped lady and say that she attacked us with her cane."

53

I worried about his mental stability and wondered how he passed the psychological test. My partner also had a morbid perspective of life. To him, if death was not the answer to all problems then it was part of the solution. His favorite thing to do was pull over mothers driving cars with children who were not wearing their seat belts.

He would politely say, "Excuse me ma'am, I stopped you because your child is not wearing a seat belt. One day your child is going to stand up and distract your attention from the road. You're going to look over at him, slam into the back of a flatbed truck and get decapitated. Your child is going to get ejected out of the window, land on some old lady's car and cause her to crash into a crosswalk full of school children. Blood and limbs are going to be lying everywhere. Then, some dog is going to come by, pick up an arm and take it home to another little kid. Is that what you want to happen?"

Usually by then, the woman would be in tears. She'd apologize and promise not to let it happen again.

Once before work, my partner walked into the locker room carrying a large black duffel bag. Curious, I asked, "What's in the bag?"

Looking around suspiciously to see if anyone else was around, he replied, "This is between us okay."

When the coast was clear, he opened the duffel bag and showed me its contents. Inside of the bag was an automatic handgun with laser sights, 200 rounds of ammo, two tear gas canisters, a gas mask and a bulletproof helmet.

"Damn man! What are you carrying all this stuff for?"

"Because I never know what might happen on the way to work between here and the freeway," he answered.

"The freeway is less than a mile away. What can possibly happen to cause you to use all this stuff?"

"I might get ambushed by fifty gang bangers. You never know. It could happen and if it does, I want to be ready."

He then told me that he had to summon up all his strength to resist the temptation to kill people. "If I ever get diagnosed with a terminal disease, I'm going to load up all my guns and drive around the city shooting gang members and people who look like they're tough. If any police officers try and stop me then I'll shoot them too." He then turned toward me and asked, "Don't you feel the same way?"

"Naw man. That's not normal. I think you need some help." I answered. "I don't want to kill anybody. I am a man of peace, love and tranquility. Man must stop wanting to destroy one another. Our ability to love is what makes us different from all other species in the universe!"

"Where did you get that from, Malcolm X? Martin Luther King? Marcus Garvey?"

"Nope. Captain Kirk from *Star Trek*. You could learn a lot by watching that show," I answered.

On more than one occasion, my partner expressed the desire to date a Black woman.

"Hey partner, how do you feel about interracial dating? I've been seriously thinking about dating out of my race and I want to know how you feel about it?"

"Well, you're a nice guy and I'm flattered but I'm already dating a woman right now, sorry," I responded.

"I don't want to date you stupid. I'm talking about a Black woman," he said.

"Oh, you scared me for a minute. If that's what you want to do then do it. I'll help you."

Standing on the corner of Western Ave. and 39th St. was a dirty, ashy, dark complexioned base head prostitute with no teeth. I stopped the patrol car directly in front of her and yelled out the window.

"Hey! Are you single?"

"Yeah, why you wanna know?" she asked.

"Because my partner wants to start dating Black women."

My partner quickly rolled up the window and tried to put his hand over my mouth.

"What in the world are you doing?" he asked.

"I'm trying to hook you up with a sister." I answered.

"I don't want no base head!"

"You've got to start somewhere. You don't think that you're going to just land you a Vanessa Williams or a Whitney Houston the first time around do you? Start here and work your way up. That's how we do it."

"You are crazy. I think you need some help," he said.

Every time a Black woman showed him some interest, he would chicken out and eat cheese, thus developing the nickname Cheezy. I seldom referred to him by his real name. I even called him Cheezy in front of citizens. Weeks later we had developed a bond. Cheezy was the only person with whom I've ever felt completely safe working.

One night, Cheezy affectionately told me that he liked me as a person. "If anyone messes with you, let me know and I'll kill them for you. LAPD employees included."

Misty eyed, I replied, "Gee, thanks. That's the nicest thing anyone's ever said to me."

Since I was the senior officer in the car by six months and had more knowledge of the division than my partner, I usually called the shots. My only career goal at this time was to eliminate a small renegade gang called the West Blvd. crips. The West Blvd. crips hung out on West Blvd. and Adams Blvd. They made it their business to shoot up the Black P-Stone bloods and the School Yard crips in Wilshire Division. Their hobbies included robbing people up and down Crenshaw Blvd., particularly at the Taco Bell on 30th St. and in front of the bank on 29th St. and Crenshaw Blvd.

My mission on them was clearly a personal vendetta. Before I became one of LA's finest, I worked at that bank and ate at that Taco Bell five days a week. On my last day working at the bank, my boss pleaded with me, "Please promise me that if you ever work in this area as a police officer you will try to do something to stop all these robberies. The police in this area don't seem to care."

As I walked out of the bank door for the last time, I promised my boss I'd return. Between homicide scenes and crime reports, Cheezy and I would patrol near the area of Adams and West Blvd. hunting for West Blvd. crips. One night we were about three blocks away when we heard several gun shots sound off. Seconds later, we received a radio call of a shooting in progress on West Blvd. With the head lights turned off, we swooped around the corner. A young gang

57

banger standing on the corner acting as lookout yelled, "One time! One time! One time is here!"

"One time" was the new generation's nickname for the police. From what I understood, the term originated from jailed inmates. Every time they would tell one of their crime stories they begin by saying, "One time..." That's only one explanation. Another is Sheriffs Deputies in the county jail always say, "I'm only going to tell you 'one time' to do something." As a result, inmates began calling all police officers "one time."

In the middle of the street I saw five gang members pushing a car. We naturally assumed the car was stolen. My partner and I quickly decided to pursue the gang member in the driver's seat because the District Attorneys' office usually only filed criminal charges on the driver of a stolen car. Within seconds of our arrival, the five gang members took off running in different directions. As planned, we ran after the gang member who was in the driver's seat.

Jetting out of the car like Carl Lewis, I was confident that I was going to catch this guy within a few yards. After all, I was twelve for twelve in catching suspects during foot pursuits, a feat equivalent to Joe Di Maggio's fifty-six game hitting streak. It was just that difficult to catch a criminal on his home turf.

The crip headed down a long driveway between two apartment buildings. The gap between the crip and me quickly closed on every stride. Seconds later the crip was in arms reach. Reaching out I grabbed him by his shirt collar and pulled his neck backwards with all of my strength. Like an equestrian pulling on the reins of a horse, the young man's head yanked back as I commanded him to stop.

Suddenly, the West Blvd. crip spun around and jammed a .380 caliber handgun into my stomach. Without having time to draw my gun, my natural instinct was to grab the gun and hold on to it for dear life.

Although everything was taking place rapidly, it appeared to be in slow motion. I felt as if my spirit had left my body, rendering my senses numb as I watched myself fight to stay alive from a distance.

"Gun!" I yelled back to my partner.

With my free hand, I delivered a hard, jaw-rattling forearm to the crip's head. Our forward momentum caused us to fall to the ground and tumble over onto our heads. When I stopped rolling, I was surprised to find his gun was tightly secured in my hand. The crip sprung back on his feet and ran down the driveway in Cheezy's direction. My partner, the elite ninja-killing machine, attempted a weak shoulder tackle on the crip. Cheezy's feeble attempt caused him to fall down while the crip bounced off him and kept running.

Once back on my feet, I quickly caught up to the crip and gave him a quick leg sweep causing him to stumble and fall. Like a raving mad dog, I turned him over, sat on his chest and began punching him in the nose repeatedly. Cheezy called my name several times and then grabbed me by my right arm.

"Hey man, take it easy," he said.

I looked at my partner with a trance like stare. For a few seconds I had no idea who he was nor did I know where I was. I looked down at the crip's bloodied face and then everything came back to me.

Damn, I almost got shot.

Even though I had just whipped on a suspect, I didn't consider myself to be a bad cop. I had just lost it for a few seconds. It was then I realized there probably weren't many bad police officers but a lot of bad partners out in the field. My partner could have stood by and watched me pound the hell out of the guy but Cheezy stepped in when he saw I was out of control. I thanked him dearly for that.

Rolling my arrestee back over onto his stomach, I cuffed him. As we had suspected, the car was stolen. During our search, we also found three more guns inside the car and several bullet holes in the door. I speculated the gang members had just completed a drive-by shooting and met some resistance. The arrestee neither denied nor confirmed my speculation.

As I sat him in the back of the patrol car, I asked the suspect if he needed medical treatment and if he wanted to make a complaint against me.

"Naw cuzz. I've been beaten up worse than this by yawl before. This ain't nothing!" he said.

Though relieved by his refusal to complain, I was somewhat disturbed that he was so accustomed to physical abuse by the police that he saw it as the norm. Once, I responded to a back-up call in the alley behind 1100 W. 43rd St. As the patrol car turned down the dark alley, I observed the figures of four people scuffling in the shadows. When my partner and I got closer, we discovered the shadows belonged to two officers and two teenage Hispanic suspects who were handcuffed on the ground. One of the suspects was bleeding profusely from his head. A handgun belonging to one of the suspects was lying in the middle of the alley.

Looking down on the injured suspect, I asked, "Are you alright? Do you need a paramedic?"

"I'm cool *homez*."

"A sergeant is on his way so if you want to make a complaint you can do it when he gets here."

Looking at me as if to ask, "Are you serious?" The gang member said, "What good would it do to complain? Who's going to believe a cholo with a fifteen-page rap sheet and on parole? I'm not a punk. I'll deal with it."

When the sergeant arrived, he asked the injured suspect, "How did you hurt your head sir?"

"I fell sir."

"Are you sure? Did these officers hit you?"

"No sir, I fell."

"Okay then, that's how I'm going to write it in my report. The blood on your head is from you falling."

There was no way I could let my arrestee walk into the station bloody. I didn't want the watch commander to ask him any questions. I figured if the suspect had time to think about it, he'd change his mind about complaining. I reached inside of the glove box and took out some old unused Mc Donald's napkins. I then wiped the blood off his face and nose.

Putting the napkin to his nose, I jokingly said, "Come on now, blow for daddy."

When word reached around the station of the West Blvd. crips' boldness, they became the target of every officer in the division. After Cheezy and I booked our arrestee the

61

atmosphere in the patrol car was not the usual loose, carefree environment it once was. The reality of death was present. Strangely enough it took another near brush with death to make me remember I had a dangerous job. Like so many other victims I never thought it could happen to me. Oddly I began to worry about which picture the department would hang on the wall if I had died. I didn't want to look goofy and have people say I died because I was goofy.

In a somber voice Cheezy said, "If you would have gotten killed tonight, I would have felt very bad but on a positive note, I would have killed him for you. If I get killed, what would you do for me?"

"If you get killed, I'll keep your name alive."

"How would you do that?" he asked.

"Well, every time I bang your girlfriend I'd say, 'this is for Cheezy. This is for Cheezy baby!"

That eased the tension somewhat as we both laughed. After the laughter evaporated, the unsatisfied presence of death again lingered inside our car.

As soon as I got home from work, I picked up the phone and called everyone I knew. My intentions were to tell each and every one of my friends and family that I loved them and was sorry for any problems I may have caused them. Unfortunately, the only thing I managed to say was, "I just called to say hello."

Some people say when a person dies in his dreams he dies in reality. That was not true for me. That night as I dreamed, I died over and over again. I saw myself lying in a casket while my mother stood over me crying. The church organist softly played "Amazing Grace," my mother's favorite song. The church was filled to capacity with sobbing friends and family. No one from the Los Angeles Police Department was in attendance. My dream concluded with the sound of Scottish bagpipes ringing in my ear. I was surprised I didn't wake up in a cold sweat like usual. Instead, I slept like a baby, peacefully and at ease as though I were dead.

The following night Cheezy and I parked our patrol car one block away from West Blvd. Climbing fences and squeezing between bushes, we sneaked into the backyard of the West Blvd. crips' hang out. Crouching down I observed about ten of the gang members standing around drinking beer in front. No guns were seen but we naturally assumed some were nearby since there was a war going on. Taking a deep breath, we counted to three and approached them with our guns drawn.

"Don't move or you're dead!"

I was stunned that the gang members not only complied with our demand but like conditioned lab rats they all lined up and assumed the "position". Holstering my gun I began searching the gang member closest to me while my partner covered me. As I searched him, the gang member glanced over his shoulder and looked down the street.

"Keep your eyes forward!" I rudely shouted.

The gang member looked forward and then did a double take to again look down the street. The gangbanger's eyes suddenly bulged, as he appeared to focus in on what he was looking at. Suddenly, he looked terrified. He looked as if he had seen a ghost. His mouth moved but no words came out.

63

"What's wrong with you? Are you retarded or something?" I asked.

The look of terror grew on his face with each second. Still holding onto the gangbanger, I glanced down the street to see what he was looking at. Down the street, a 1978 Oldsmobile without headlights was slowly coming in our direction. My eyes enlarged when I saw the front passenger wearing a red bandanna tied around his face like a western cowboy. To make matters worse the blood was leaning out of the window holding a shotgun and continuously scanning the street for prey. Spotting the crips and assuming Cheezy and I were one of them, he directed the driver to our location.

"It's the P-Stones. Drive by! Drive by!" one of the crips yelled.

All of the crips dropped their hands and broke out running in different directions. Déjà vu', my early childhood days flashed in my mind. I had been there before. It had been ten years since I last ran from a drive-by shooting.

Maybe it is my fate to die in a drive-by shooting after all.

While everyone else ran, the two dumbfounded officers stood out like sitting ducks. In the police academy, instead of officers being taught to run like hell, we were taught to take cover behind a solid object when shot were fired. This time as always, there was nowhere to take cover.

Just as the car came within three houses of us, the passenger yelled, "Stop the car! One time, One time!"

The driver suddenly slammed on the brakes, put the car in reverse and wildly sped backwards down the street. The car crashed into the curb in its attempt to escape. Cheezy and

64

I were too far away from our car to do anything about it. All we could do was put out a broadcast of the car and hope the air unit or another patrol unit picked it up. No one did. The drive-by shooters disappeared in the distance.

For two nights in a row death not only knocked at my front door but it had rung my back doorbell and tried to sneak through the side window as well. I began to wonder if I would make it through the summer without shooting someone or getting shot. It was only by the grace of God I survived those two days.

Again, when the night was over, I was forced to deal with the scariest part of the job. I had no choice but to go home and reflect on the day's events and my early childhood experiences. As already mentioned, I was once a victim of a drive-by shooting when I was in my teens. For this reason, hatred toward all gang members burned deep within my heart. Practically every party I went to from junior high to high school was marred by gang violence of some kind.

Even though my neighborhood was considered a safe place to live, Friday and Saturday nights could prove to be quite dangerous. Windsor Hills and the surrounding neighborhoods had a reputation throughout the city as being the place to party. There was always a party going on somewhere in the neighborhood. Gang members from all over the city cruised the neighborhood looking for parties to crash and if they couldn't get in, they'd shoot it up. One night, my buddies and I were walking to a party just a few blocks away from my house at the Park Hills Community Church Recreation Center.

My friends and I were only three blocks away from our destination when we realized a blue Monte Carlo with darkly tinted windows had circled the block a couple of times. My friends and I nonchalantly continued to walk to the party as if nothing was wrong. We knew there was no way we could be mistaken for gang members. We were all wearing cheap multicolored fake silk shirts, polyester slacks, Stacey Adams shoes and sporting shag haircuts. We were wannabe pimps at best.

As a precaution, in the event we were approached, we devised a game plan. First, we would play it cool and wait to see if we would be asked the magic question. If we were, then the fellas would split up and run in different directions. Finally, we would meet up at our friend Terry Jr's house around the corner.

The driver of the Monte Carlo turned into a driveway several feet in front of us. The car came to a stop across the sidewalk. We had no choice but to pass in front of the car. Four hard looking gangbangers exited the car wearing long coats. One of them had his right hand stuck in his jacket as if he was concealing a gun.

Smiling, but looking cool, I cordially nodded my head upward and said, "What's up?"

"Nothing," one of them answered.

Then the gang member coldly looked straight in my eyes and asked, "What set you from cuzz?"

That was the magic question my friends and me were hoping not to hear. I knew if I said I didn't gang bang, then I would get shot for being a punk. It was more than obvious we were not gang affiliated. If I had tried to fake it and picked a

66

gang, I could get shot for lying or being the enemy. Basically, my friends and I were damned if we did and damned if we didn't. That's why we ran like hell.

As planned, we split up in separate directions. I hopped the nearest fence and hid in some bushes. From where I was hiding, I could see the gangbanger with his hand inside of his jacket was now holding a .38 caliber revolver in his right hand.

"Why didn't you shoot?" One of them asked the gunman.

"Damn! Them marks jetted out so fast that I didn't know which one to shoot."

Frustrated, the gang bangers jumped into their car and sped off. When the coast was clear, I nervously crawled out of my hiding place and ran to Terry Jr's house. The rest of my crew was already there. We told Dirty Terry what had just happened. Dirty Terry's face didn't change expressions but his eyes dilated with excitement. He calmly told my friends and me not to worry and that he would handle it. Dirty Terry loaded up his .357 magnum revolver and sat on his front porch drinking a beer, waiting for the gang members to return. The gang members were fortunate they didn't return. Dirty Terry looked terribly disappointed when they didn't.

Dirty Terry was the first person I had ever seen willingly want to confront gang members. The look in his eyes made an ever-lasting impression in my mind.

The next weekend, my friends and I were not so lucky. Walking home late one night after a party, we were approached by two guys in an older model Oldsmobile Cutlass, also with darkly tinted windows. The driver slowly cruised along side of my nervous friends and me as we walked.

"Hey fellas!" the passenger said. "Where's the party at?"

"Sorry, you missed it. It was jamming," my friend said.

"Okay then, since we missed it, I want you guys to give us some gas money so we can get home," the passenger said in a serious tone of voice.

I was tired of running from gang members. My new Stacey Adams shoes were so scuffed up from being chased home they looked like I'd been playing soccer in them. Besides, Dirty Terry had given me the confidence to stand up and fight.

Sticking my chest out, I sarcastically asked, "If we don't give you any money, what are you going to do, shoot us?"

I didn't get a chance to finish my sentence before the shooting started. Like lightning streaking through the night, muzzle flashes streamed out the car window in our direction. Pop! Pop! Pop! gunshots rang out. Running as fast as I could, I dove into the nearby bushes. Three more shots rang out before the car sped away. As I climbed out of the bushes, I checked myself for bullet holes and missing parts. Fortunately, I was all there.

Unfortunately, one of my friends was lying on his back in a pool of blood. He had been shot twice in the leg. Luckily, he was not seriously hurt but his promising high school baseball career had to be put on hold until he could walk again.

I was normally an obedient kid but this time I was so mad that I went home and tried to jimmy the lock on my father's desk drawer where he kept his guns. It was a good thing I didn't know what I was doing. If I had, there was a strong possibility I would have killed someone or have been killed trying.

The next night Cheezy and I decided to leave well enough alone. We had almost gotten ourselves killed two nights in a row in front of the same apartment building. We were normally gun-ho but on this night we mutually decided not to go anywhere near that apartment building. While driving around the hood trying to avoid trouble, we observed two men standing in an alley. One man was wearing dark clothing and pointing a handgun at the other. The other man stood stiffly with both hands held high in the air. He had a look of terror shadowed across his face. Cheezy and I both knew we had stumbled upon a robbery in progress. Normally, I would have been honored to be presented with this opportunity of excitement but not this time. The adrenaline rush wasn't there!

When the robber saw the Black and White driving up, he quickly dashed between the houses. I looked at Cheezy and Cheezy looked over at me. Neither one of us moved. It was obvious neither one of us wanted to run after the suspect fearing our luck had run out. Needless to say, the suspect got away.

As one of my old training officers used to say, "That's job security. Letting criminals get away just insures us that we have a job tomorrow."

No matter how hard we tried to avoid danger, we couldn't. Even the simplest and most basic calls turned out to be dangerous. Cheezy and I responded to a disturbing the peace call near the Southwest police station on Dalton Ave. We apprehensively took our time getting to the call

69

because we figured by the time we got there the problem would have resolved itself. When we arrived, I saw a disc jockey and his crew running to their cars carrying their stereo equipment and records. The owner of the residence came over to the patrol car.

"The party is over officers. My son had a birthday party and some gangbangers unexpectedly showed up and turned the party out. I'm making everybody go home officers. Thanks for coming by."

Turning to me, Cheezy whispered, "Just like we planned. Case closed!"

Just then, a car full of teenagers pulled up next to the Black and White. The occupants in the car pointed down the street and hysterically told us a gang member was coming toward us with an AK-47 rifle.

I radioed for back up and then proceeded in the gang member's direction. Just as the teenagers had said, we observed a gang member walking down the street with a large gun in both hands. The gunman looked at us and hesitated for a second. Then with a sudden burst of energy he took off running down an alley still carrying his weapon. Cheezy pressed his foot on the accelerator and headed after the gunman.

"Hit him! Hit him! Run the knucklehead over Cheezy! Get him!" I wildly screamed as the patrol car sped toward the suspect. The gang member stopped, raised his rifle up to a firing position and pointed it at us. Fortunately, the headlights on the patrol car blinded him and caused him to drop his gun and shield his eyes. Through the darkness, the suspect disappeared in a backyard.

70

Luckily the air unit spotted him running into his own house on the next street. After an eight-hour standoff with SWAT, the suspect surrendered. Inside the house Cheezy and I found two more AK-47s and several handguns.

That morning, a detective walked up and told me the other detectives were betting we wouldn't make it to the end of summer without getting shot. That was such a nice thing for him to say! Police officers were the most negative people on earth. They always wished the worst on everybody. Just in case the detective was right in his prediction, the following Sunday I went to church and prayed extra hard.

Several weeks later on a Wednesday the department transfer list was posted in the hallway of the station. To my amazement, I saw Cheezy's name on the top of the list. I cornered my partner in the locker room and demanded an explanation.

"I'm sorry but I'm tired of this south end crap. I'm tired of hearing people calling me a White, racist, Rodney King beaten cop. I'm not like that. I've stopped you from hurting people. I'm going to North Hollywood Division where the citizens are nicer and appreciate the police. I'm just tired of everything, the pitiful Southwest sergeants and every night eating Taco Bell or at greasy hamburger stands. In the valley, the food is not only better it's free. The eating-places down here won't give us a cent off. I can't take this anymore!"

I knew exactly what he meant. Often, I had entertained the idea of leaving the division myself but as a neighborhood cop, I felt a sense of duty to stay in the neighborhood. In the back of my mind I wondered whether or not Cheezy left the division out of the fear of dying as we were projected to do or if

71

he was just tired. Cheezy and I said our good-byes and promised to keep in touch.

As a result of my fear of dying, my method of police work changed dramatically as I uncharacteristically began taking personal interest in certain young gang members. Prior to my revelation I seriously tried to avoid getting personally involved with any hardheads because either by death or incarceration, gang members were literally here today and gone tomorrow. It was easier for me to psychologically cope with that disturbing fact if I just referred to them as knuckleheads and idiots.

One time one of my partners and I spotted a young kid around ten years old standing on a corner with an older teenager about eighteen years old. Pulling over my partner stopped to chat with the youths. The first thing I noticed was that they were both dressed down in gang type clothing which meant, baggy brown khaki pants, a red Pendleton shirt and a pair of black tennis shoes with bright red shoe laces.

I was only concerned for the well being of the ten year old, because I felt the older fellow was already lost to the corruption of the streets.

Pointing to the younger kid, I asked the other, "Who is this?"

"That's my *peoples*," he answered.

"What's he doing standing on the corner at two in the morning?" I shouted.

"He's with me. We just chillin. Why, what's the problem?" the older one asked with hostility.

72

"The problem is that it's two in the morning and he needs to be at home. Take him home now or I'll find a reason to take you to jail."

I would have taken the kid home myself but I knew talking to his parents wouldn't have made a difference anyway. My limited experience had taught me if the parents had cared, the child wouldn't have been out there in the first place. For some strange reason, the two stuck in my mind. Every night I would see the two hanging out together.

Leaning out of the window, I would yell, "Take care of the little guy and get him home by dark or your mine!"

The older one would smile and reply, "Don't worry I will."

My relationship with the kid seemed to grow until one night when I leaned out of the window to speak I noticed they both appeared to be rigid and tense. Looking into the older ones eyes, I could tell something was wrong. My heart began to beat faster and faster and my palms began to sweat.

Whispering to my partner, I said, "The older one is packing. Let's do it."

Slamming on the brakes the Black and White came to a screeching stop. Jumping out of the car I drew my gun with confidence and enthusiasm. Simultaneously the two bolted in separate directions. I gave chase to the older one through some apartment buildings. I lost sight of him for a few seconds but then caught up to him in a fenced area.

Innocently stopping he put his hands up. I quickly handcuffed and searched my catch for a weapon. He was clean. My partner then checked the bushes directly behind the gang member and found a loaded revolver lying between the

73

limbs. We knew under the circumstances the case would be dismissed because we never actually saw the gang member with the gun. We could have lied and said we saw the suspect with the gun but I believed in telling the truth or that's what I tried to convince myself. If the gang member had been one of the typical loud mouth, beer and bud breath hostile idiots whom I usually dealt with, the decision to tell the truth wouldn't have come so easily. On a positive note, we at least removed a gun from the street.

While booking the gang member at the station, I gave him the old "gang banging is not worth it" speech. Hopefully, the youth would be the one out of a thousand gang members who listened and changed. I used to make that speech on a regular basis until I started losing hope. At first I thought I was able to identify with all youths in the community. I learned the hard way that even though I grew up and still resided in the community, I couldn't. How could I empathize with a child who had never seen his father or whose mother was strung out on drugs and all his brothers in prison? How could I realistically give sound advice to someone when I didn't fully understand his problem? It was more than a Black thang, it was an experience thang and I was an outsider.

"You need to seriously consider giving up banging. You're gonna either wind up dead or in jail. This case will probably get dropped but now that I know you carry a gun, I'm going to stop and search you every single day that I see you."

Three days later, I received a radio call of a drive-by shooting. As I listened carefully to the call on my radio, the address rang out in my head like a bell. The address of the call was on the same corner the two youths hung out on every night. My stomach knotted up as my partner and I got closer to our destination. I was hoping, almost praying, it wasn't one of the brothers. I would have prayed but I didn't know if it was appropriate for an officer to do so on-duty.

As we drove up, I noticed a large crowd standing behind a perimeter of yellow crime scene tape. Two units had already arrived at the scene before us and were attempting to control the crowd. Making my way through the crowd, I saw the little brother sitting on the ground crying and clenching onto his out stretched, blood soaked older brother.

The older gang member's eyes rolled back into his head and his bullet riddled body shook with convulsions. Several police officers stood over the victim and his little brother.

Pointing to the victim and laughing, one officer said, "Look at him. He's flapping up and down like a fish out of water."

"No, he's just going through an exorcism," another added.

"You're both wrong. He's break dancing" someone else said.

Grabbing the kid by the arm, I lead him away from his dying brother and the insensitive officers. I bent down and half-heartedly told the kid, "Don't worry. Your brother is going to be fine."

Needless to say, he died on the way to the hospital. Later on that night, I told the officers who were at the scene that I thought they could have been a little more sensitive at the homicide scene.

75

"That was messed up! The way you guys made jokes about the victim in front of his brother was wrong," I said.

"So what. Maybe the little jerk will get traumatized and give up gang banging," an officer said.

"It's your fault that he's dead."

"What do you mean it's my fault?" I asked.

"If you wouldn't have arrested him and took his gun away from him he might have been able to defend himself against his killer. You made the sucker a sitting duck."

"Hey, good job. You should get credit for the kill!"

"You guys are sick!"

The conversation did make me wonder if the gangbanger would still be alive if I had not taken his gun away and threatened to search him every day. My early days as a young naive police officer were really something to consider and cherish. When I first came on the job, my goal was to help people and make my community a better place to live. I figured I could use my education and communication skills to persuade young adults they could be a productive part of society. After only four short years of patrolling in South Central Los Angeles, instead of teaching others and conveying a positive message to youths, I was taught a lesson in reality.

For a minute I felt badly but like almost every other police officer on the department, I finally concluded, "Oh well, things happen!" There was no room in my already disturbed mind to worry about the gang member's death, especially since I knew I would probably have to deal with a retaliation death the next day. The odds were that I would most likely know the next victim as well. I deducted that the best thing I as a patrol officer could do, was try not to get too attached to anyone I

76

came in contact with on-duty, especially a gang member. Being friends with a gang member was like having a gold fish as a friend. An officer couldn't get too attached because as soon as the weather got hot, gang members started dying.

ENOUGH IS ENOUGH!

"What if I've just been raped by two buck Black guys and some female (officer) shows up? What is she going to do?"

Former LAPD Detective Mark Fuhrman. (Based on transcripts used by the O.J Simpson defense lawyers)

Four months later as a skilled officer, I was moved to the mid P.M. watch, which was from 6:00pm to 3:00am. The officers on this watch considered themselves to be the elite officers in the division. On mid P.M watch, we got out of roll call right when all the action started happening and left when things started dying down.

This time, I was assigned to work with an overweight blonde female officer. Whoever said, "Blondes have more fun," certainly wasn't a police officer. She sternly laid down the rules the first day we worked together.

"I don't go into 'The Jungle' nor do I run after people. I don't deal with gang members and I don't do traffic stops," she said.

"What in the hell do you do?" I asked.

"Look! Let me make this perfectly clear. The only reason that I'm working in this division is because working in a south end division looks good in your personnel file. I want to finish my year here without a personnel complaint and without being killed. Then, I want to go back to the valley and take the sergeants' test." She explained.

The frightening thing was that someday she would probably become a sergeant. The department traditionally promoted officers who had no interest in doing police work, no concern for helping minority citizens and who were afraid of their own shadow. Once these officers were promoted, they were then assigned to work in a south end division where they didn't want to work as a patrol officer.

Needless to say, my new partner and I didn't get along. Every evening before roll call, I'd slip into the watch commander's office and change the lineup board so I wouldn't have to work with her. I didn't ask the watch commander for permission to change the board because I didn't want the reputation of not being a team player or not being able to work with women. My partner's outlook didn't cause me to think negatively about female officers because I knew of some male officers who would also refuse to patrol "The Jungle." I also knew of male officers who would not run after people or climb a fence to save their own life. I just viewed our situation as a conflict of interest. As it turned out, I was not the only one who didn't want to work with her. Sometimes her name would get switched around on the lineup board at least five times until it went in a full circle back to me.

Sometimes the atmosphere in our patrol car would be so tense and quiet, not a word would be spoken all day. It was a real drag knowing I would be working with someone I didn't care for or converse with. Sitting next to this large woman in a tight and confining patrol car for eight hours was murder. Finally, one day it all came to a head.

Out of nowhere she blurted, "Look! If you don't want to work with me then just say so!"

79

Calmly, I responded, "Why on earth wouldn't I want to work with you?"

"Because some people just don't like working with women. They don't feel like we can do the job."

"There isn't a doubt in my mind that you can do the job. You just don't do it the way I do it, that's all. It's nothing against you personally. I think you're a nice person."

"Thanks. It doesn't matter anyway because I'm going to get the hell out of this division as soon as I can."

One month later, on a Wednesday, her name was on the transfer list to a valley division. I was then assigned to work with another female officer no one wanted to work with. My new partner's appearance was not very appealing. Every uniform she owned was too small and badly stitched up from numerous rips. She never shined her shoes and according to her, she was always having a bad hair day.

I didn't have a problem working with a female but I did wonder why I kept getting them as partners. I believed it was probably because I was the only one who didn't voice my complaint.

THE ONLY FEMALE PARTNER I EVER COMPLAINED AGAINST WAS A BOURGEOIS BLACK FEMALE TRAINING OFFICER AT WEST LA DIVISION. On our first night working together she told me, "Since we are both Black, I want you to feel like you can tell me anything. Feel free to talk about whatever you want. I will keep it between us because Blacks need to stick together on this job."

I could imagine the difficulties my Nubian sister must have experienced while trying to become a police officer. She had to fight the stereotypes of being Black and a woman, which was considered to be a double negative in some veterans' eyes. Becoming a new Black female training officer in a predominately White division must have been added pressure.

That night, at about four in the morning, we responded to a disturbing the peace call near the UCLA campus. As we drove up I could hear music blasting from an apartment two blocks away. Sternly knocking on the door with my metal flashlight, I identified myself as a police officer. Three drunk, White UCLA students stared at the Black LAPD officers through a window. Shouting over the loud music, I politely asked them to turn off the music.

With slurred speech, one of the them asked, "Who are you?"

Politely, I answered, "The police sir."

"How do I know that you're really the police? You could have stolen that uniform. You guys don't look like the normal police officers that patrol this area," he said.

Finally, after five minutes of trying to convince them we were really police officers, the little jerks turned off the music. Back in the car my training officer asked, "I don't get it? Why do you think they refused to believe we were police officers?"

I felt comfortable with my new training officer because she was young and Black. I was glad she had asked that question. I figured that since we were both Black, we had that Black thang going on or as White people say, "We had a positive aura in the car." Like a fool, I decided to let my hair down and vent my frustrations.

81

I gladly answered her question. "They didn't want to believe us because they didn't think LAPD would allow two Black police officers to work together at 4:30 a.m. in the Brentwood area. If we were White, I don't think we would have had that problem," I said.

I then went on to tell her how irritated I got when White victims would look at me and say, "The guy that robbed me was your height and weight with a build and hair cut like yours. He looked just like you!" They might as well have said, "You all look alike." In fact, one of my other training officers jokingly asked me if I was robbing people before work.

I continued, "That is why I will never live in a White neighborhood because at any given time, I could get swept away by the police and booked for at least fifty different robberies based on the way I look. I became a police officer to help my community and the West LA area is not my damn community! One day I'm going to return to my community and help my people," I concluded.

I felt relieved. To me, that little speech was as big as Dr. Martin Luther King's "I Have a Dream" speech.

My new training officer never said another word to me for the rest of the night. The next day, the captain of the division called me into his office. The captain of West LA Division was in his first year as a patrol captain. He was a tall, thin, middle-aged, Black man with a heavy southern backwoods drawl. Curiously walking into the captain's office I saw the captain resting comfortably behind a huge wooden desk. Four angry looking, red-faced sergeants stood up against the far wall of the office. I had no idea why I was there, but judging by the look on their faces, it didn't look good.

82

The captain told me to take a seat. "So, I understand that you don't like White people and you think that the fine citizens of West Los Angeles are prejudiced."

I was speechless. A large lump grew in my throat as though I was about to cry. I couldn't believe that my training officer suckered me. When I was younger, I had heard my brothers and sisters talk about how Black people were their own worst enemies. Now, I was experiencing it for myself.

As the captain yelled at a frightened rookie and called me a racist, beads of sweat dripped from my forehead and streamed down my back from nervousness. Half way through the captain's hour and a half long speech, my body became drenched in sweat.

"Do you know what your problem is son? Now a day, you young rebellious kids graduate from college and think you're not supposed to take orders from White people anymore. Remember this, as long as you live, you're going to have to take orders from White people. I'm the captain of this division but the commander is White. It's never going to change," he said.

You sorry, Uncle Tom, please don't fire me, I thought. *I can't trust a police officer no matter what color he is,* I also thought.

By now, the captain's words were going in one ear and passing out the other. I began to wonder if I was assigned to West LA Division by chance or because on paper I looked like a West LA type of Negro. After all, I was bused to a predominately White junior high and high school. When I traveled home after school on the R.T.D bus, I had to look tough enough so the older White racist kids wouldn't attack me on the bus stop. On the contrary, as I rode through the city of Inglewood, I had to look as non-gang affiliated as possible. I did this by removing all of my blue clothing so the Inglewood Family bloods wouldn't jump me.

The most disappointing thing about what was taking place was that both my training officer and the captain were active members of the Black police officers association called the O.J.B. Association. The O.J.B. Association was named after the late Oscar Joel Bryant who was the first Black LAPD police officer killed in the line of duty. It was founded with the purpose of helping Black officers unite and fight against discrimination. Because of my Black captain and training officer I never joined the association. I didn't feel comfortable with the association, knowing its members were hypocrites.

For the next two weeks, my training officer verbally abused me in front of citizens. Once, she cursed me out because I informed her she was driving in the wrong direction to a call.

"Damnit, I'm your training officer! I tell you which way to go!" she angrily yelled.

Finally, I decided enough was enough. I felt dejected and distraught. One night before going to work, I handed my mother an envelope with two hundred and fifty dollars inside. At the time, this was the exact bail amount for the charge of battery against a police officer. I decided if my training officer yelled at me, I was going to beat the hell out of her.

With a serious look on my face, I said to my mother, "Here mom, take this money. You might have to bail me out of jail tonight. I'm sick of this job. Before I quit, I'm going to hurt my training officer."

"Don't be silly! Use your head and think about what you're about to do," she replied.

Pausing for a moment, I knew my mother was right. I was not using my head. I walked back into my room and got my savings book out of the drawer.

Handing the savings book to my mother, I said, "You are right, I wasn't using my head. Here is some more money. I might have to shoot her."

As I walked out of my house, I could hear my mother cursing me for everything she could think of.

Once at the station, I approached the evening as if I was a boxer preparing for a big fight. In the locker room, I stretched the muscles in my back and arms until I developed a light sweat. As usual, after roll call, my training officer tore into me as soon as we pulled away from the station.

"Tonight, I want you to write six tickets. You better not screw up but I know you will because you can't do anything right!" she yelled.

I immediately pulled the car over and unfastened my seatbelt.

"What in the hell are you doing?" she asked.

Pointing my finger in her face and turning my pumped up body toward her, I calmly said, "I'm not putting up with your crap any more. If you say one more word to me, I'm gonna slap the taste out your mouth! Do you understand?" I then smiled and said, "Now go tell the captain that!"

My training officer just sat there with a blank stare on her face. In a faint and meek voice, she politely asked me to drive her back to the station. That wasn't the response I had hoped for.

"What did you call me?" I asked.

Clearing her throat, she replied, "Nothing."

Although I was still angry, thoughts of confusion and doubt clouded my mind as I wondered if I had done the right thing. As a new kid, I had just broken the cardinal LAPD rule by talking back to a training officer. Obeying a training officer was more important to a rookie than biding any chapter in the LAPD manual. Without any question, I knew the rest of my probation was going to be extremely rough. Everybody I'd work with would go out of his or her way to give me a hard time and they did.

When the captain got wind of what I did, he took me off the streets and ordered me to work in the station jail, which held approximately seventy-five people overnight until the LA County Sheriffs Department transferred them to court. I figured the captain would keep me in there until he could devise a plan to get rid of me permanently. Rumors spread fast throughout the LAPD. When I got home, I had at least ten phone calls on my answering machine ranging from, "I heard that you put your training officer in a choke hold", to "I heard that you made your training officer get out of the car on the freeway."

It became obvious to me as a rookie officer; the LAPD was not all it was cracked up to be. There was supposed to be a code of silence. Officers were not supposed to run and tell the captain what was said in the patrol car. The LAPD was supposed to be a family, brothers and sisters against civilians. I found none of that to be true.

Since becoming a police officer, I began to dislike police officers more than before I became one. I learned the hard way that a police officer's on-duty personality usually does not change much from his off-duty personality. For the most part, if a police officer is a jerk on-duty, then there is a good chance the officer is also a nimrod to his or her coworkers, spouse, and children. Even though my training officer didn't make a very good impression on me, I still didn't develop hatred toward female officers like other male officers.

While still on probation at West LA Division, I briefly worked with another female training officer. She was a thin White woman with a squeaky, high-pitched voice. Not only was she very knowledgeable she also took the time to talk to me and explain how unfair the department was to some officers. She then told me she also had some bad experiences on the job because of her gender.

One time an older veteran officer approached me. He spoke of my training officer. "I feel sorry for you because you have to work with that woman! She's worthless!"

It became clear that sexism was far more openly discussed and practiced in LAPD than racism. There were many male officers who didn't like working with women. They firmly believed having a woman as a partner was a safety liability. It was a general consensus among most men that women didn't come on the job for the same reasons as men. The consensus was women usually came on the job just to get paid. They usually tried to get out of the field as quickly as possible by promoting to an inside position. If they couldn't promote out of patrol then they would get out of patrol by getting pregnant.

87

Male officers generally had big egos and usually came on the job for the action. Male officers were more likely not to back down from potential physical confrontations because of their ego. That was why Chief Williams stated he wanted to increase the population of female police officers by forty percent. This comment infuriated many officers who thought female officers were worthless.

Sadly, I once overheard a veteran training officer say, "The only purpose a woman has as a police officer is to give her male partner oral sex in between radio calls."

MY NEW PARTNER WAS A TWO-YEAR VETERAN who grew up in a White upper middle-class neighborhood in racist Orange County. She didn't request Southwest Division. She came against her will as I had to the West LA Division. I wondered whom she had pissed off to have gotten transferred to "South Worst" division. Surprisingly, she was a graduate of USC with a degree in child psychology.

"If you have a degree in child psychology, why did you want to be a police officer?" I asked.

"Because my fiancée was a cop. Listening to his stories made me interested."

"So when are you guys getting married?"

"We aren't. The jerk married his partner!" she angrily replied.

"Don't get happy because that's not going to happen with us."

"I wouldn't marry you if you were the last man on this earth!"

Every night, my new partner and I fought like husband and wife. She refused to believe I knew more about the LAPD manual than she did. If I mentioned an updated amendment to the manual she would arrogantly say, "I don't think the manual says that. I've never read that." She would then go to the station and look it up. After she would find out I was right, she would pout all night. I would then rub it in by calling her "Ms. Know-it-all."

I was shocked by her work performance. She turned out to be one of the hardest working partners I ever had. Together, as a male and female duo, we statistically lead the watch in felony arrests, calls handled, reports taken, and foot pursuits. It seemed like every time we turned a corner we saw a felony crime-taking place. As basketball players say, "We were in a zone!" The difference was, my partner's and my zone could have gotten us killed.

My new partner had one serious character flaw. I had to constantly remind her to stop belittling our arrestees by making unnecessary snide remarks such as, "I know your mother wishes you would have died at birth", "We are wasting our time arresting you because you're going to die soon", and "Do the world a favor and kill yourself." She also had a very bad habit of being rude and sarcastic to victims.

One time, we responded to a radio call of a robbery that just occurred. The victim was a single twenty-three year old Black woman with six children. The woman was robbed of her whole check while she was walking to the grocery store with her children. My partner sat at the woman's dining room table and asked her the necessary information we needed to complete a report.

"I need to know your age and business address ma'am," my partner said.

"I'm twenty-three and I don't have a business address. I'm unemployed right now," the woman answered.

"Geez! You started young. I guess you've never had the time to work because you're always having babies. If you don't work, how do you feed all your kids?"

"I'm on welfare."

My partner almost jumped out of her seat in anger when she heard the victim's answer. "You mean to tell me that I'm supporting all these kids? I guess you've never heard of birth control before. Are you using it now?"

The woman seemed embarrassed by her question. She began to appear nervous as though she was being interrogated for a crime she committed against the officer questioning her. Before the woman could answer, I interrupted her.

"Excuse me but can you hurry up and finish the report so we can get on to our next call?" I asked my partner.

"Hold on. We're talking girl talk here," she replied.

"She doesn't want you to know her business. That stuff is personal."

"Oh she doesn't mind," my partner told me. She then turned back to the woman and asked, "Do they all have the same fathers?"

"Three of them do."

"I bet none of them have jobs either. That's pathetic!"

I felt my partner's questions were totally out of line and unprofessional. As public servants we were not there to humiliate the woman and put her down because she was on welfare. I walked over to my partner and snatched the report out of her hand.

"Give me that! If you don't want to take the report then I will. I don't have all day to sit around and listen to you play Oprah Winfrey. I've got criminals to catch," I told her.

She snatched the report back and said, "Give that back! I'll take the report. Chill out, will ya?"

She then calmed down and continued to take the report. After the report was completed we walked toward the front door of the victim's apartment. Before we left the victim asked, "Is this it? Are you guys going to go look for the guy? So what shall I do about my money?"

"Well, you can start by finding yourself a job. Sorry, there's nothing else that we can do for you. Besides, some base head has probably smoked up all your money by now anyway." She answered with a smirk on her face.

As we walked back to the patrol car, my partner sarcastically said, "There you go. She would make a perfect girlfriend for you. You'd have a readymade family."

"Shut your mouth! Why in the hell are you always so annoying? I see why nobody wants to work with you!"

"Oh yeah, like you're so awesome. I don't see anybody standing in line to work with you either. Everybody is afraid you're going to beat somebody to death and they don't want to be around when it happens."

"All I know is that I got stuck with you cause nobody else can deal with your mouth, Ms. Know-it-all," I came back.

"You're just upset because I was messing with your woman that's all. You know you're gonna creep back over here when you get off work. You can tell me. I won't tell," she said with a smile. "Just remember to eat before you come because she doesn't have any money to buy food. I bet she smoked it up in her cocaine pipe."

"Maybe that's what you need to lose some weight! Maybe you should stop doing step aerobics and start smoking crack," I came back.

This was not an isolated incident nor was I the only one who had a hard time dealing with it. Her only explanation for her behavior was she hated everything about the division. Oddly, I *kind of* knew exactly what she meant. Sometimes I was also guilty of being rude but nowhere near as out of line as she was daily. My sarcasm came in spurts, on bad days, when hungry and with real idiots. I never picked on nice citizens until they made me angry.

I remember losing my cool one Christmas morning. It was early and the streets were damp from a morning drizzle. Around 2 a.m., my partner and I received a radio call of a family dispute near Halldale Ave. and 27th St.

As soon as the call was broadcast, my partner asked, "Why are we going to a family dispute at 2 a.m.? It's Christmas for God sakes. Why aren't these people sleep?"

I was not overly concerned with the call. I was in a mellow mood as I looked out of the window and day dreamed about my childhood Christmas experiences.

Stepping out of the car my partner placed her hand on her holstered gun and carefully looked around. "Be careful. This could be an ambush. A Christmas day massacre," she said.

While I tactically took cover behind an old early English style pillar, my partner walked up to the front door of the

92

residence and quietly tried to listen to the conversation that was taking place. Several seconds later, my partner was partially satisfied that we weren't going to get ambushed. She then rang the doorbell.

Ding! Dong!

"Who is it?" a voice asked from inside the residence.

It's the police!" my partner answered.

From my position, I could see the curtains move and a face peer through the window. The voice then moved to the front door. "Just a minute. Let me open the door," the voice replied.

I then heard keys jingling, locks turning, and chains clanging for what appeared to be five minutes. Finally the door opened. A woman in her mid forties, wearing a nightgown and rollers in her hair stood in the doorway.

"Good morning officer," the woman said, "Come in."

"What's the problem ma'am?" my partner asked.

The woman opened the door wider and said, "Come inside and I'll explain it to you."

"Why don't you tell me what's going on first, and then maybe I'll come in?"

"Officer, I'd rather tell you inside. I don't want my neighbors to know all my business."

"Look ma'am, I don't like walking into stranger's homes blind. Either you tell me now or I'm leaving!"

"Can't we just go inside and talk? Please!" she asked.

Turning away, my partner politely said, "Good night ma'am, call us when you're ready to talk."

I could see that things had gotten off to a bad start. Leaving my position, I walked up to the door. "Hold up partner. I'll check it out."

I carefully stepped into the doorway and gazed around the room. Standing a few feet from the door were two young children dressed in pajamas. I then looked back and motioned for my partner to enter. Once we were inside, the woman quickly closed the door.

"How can I help you ma'am?" I asked.

"Well, these children are my sister's children. I've been taking care of them since they were born. My sister is strung out on crack. Before tonight I hadn't seen her in two months. Tonight she came over to borrow some money and I told her that I was going to get legal custody of the children. She got upset and now she wants to take them away from here. I told her that she couldn't take them so she called you guys."

In the shadows at the back of the room I could see a grotesque figure quickly moving from one room to another.

"Well ma'am, legally they are her children so she can take them if she wants. If you think they are going to be mistreated then there is a number you can call," my partner said.

Crying, the woman screamed, "What, you're not going to do anything? I should have known. You guys don't protect and serve no damn body!" Turning to me, she said, "I know you can do something if you wanted."

My partner stopped the woman. "Don't start that with us lady. I already told you that there isn't anything we can do."

"So you're going to let her take those children to a rock house on Christmas?"

"You don't know that she is going to do that. Besides if you would have taken care of business, this wouldn't have happened. You should have called the Department of Children's Services years ago. I'm sick of people not taking care of business and then expecting the police to do it for them," she shouted.

While my partner scolded the woman, I kneeled down and spoke to the children.

"Hey, what are your names?" I asked.

"My name is Tiffany," the little girl answered.

"My name is John," the boy told me.

"How old are you guys?"

Smiling, the boy said, "I'm five and my sister is four."

The little girl smiled and said, "Did you know that Santa Claus is coming tonight?"

My heart shot up into my throat. I felt sorry for the children. *Children shouldn't be subjected to this kind of mental anguish anytime of year*, I thought.

Standing back up, I said, "Let me talk to your sister and see if we can reach a compromise." Shouting to the figure in the back of the room, I asked, "Can you come over here for a second ma'am? I need to talk to you."

"Talk to me, for what? I didn't do nothing," she answered.

When she stepped out of the shadows, I could see that her clothes were torn and dirty. Her hair was standing straight up as if it hadn't been combed in months. Her thin, frail body reeked of a musty odor.

95

"Let's step outside and talk," I said.

I closed the door behind us as we stepped outside. "What's the real problem here? Why are you taking your kids out of a warm house and into the rain on Christmas morning?"

"I don't have a problem. My sister has a problem. Those are my kids and I'm taking them," she insisted.

"How about this, why don't you let them stay until the sun comes up and it stops raining," I suggested.

"I ain't waiting till nothing! I'm taking them now!"

"Don't you care about them?" I asked.

The woman didn't answer me. "You're only taking them now because you know if your sister gets legal custody of them, you won't get your county check. No check, no dope right?"

The woman pushed me aside and yelled, "Get the heck out of my way. I'm leaving and I'm taking my kids with me!"

I impulsively grabbed the woman by her nappy hair and pushed her down on the wet grass. Putting my foot on her neck, I said, "If you don't care about your children then I don't give a damn about you. You're not taking those kids anywhere. If you try, I'm gonna hurt you now and every other time I see you. I'll also tell everybody around here that you're giving me information about drug sales." Releasing my foot from her neck, I shouted, "Get out of here!"

As the base head stood up, I gave her a swift kick in the butt. Standing up, she turned toward me and looked me in the eye as though she was contemplating fighting back.

96

"I'm gonna sue you!" she shouted as she ran down the street.

I stood on the sidewalk and watched the woman round the corner. I then walked back inside the house and interrupted my partner who was still scolding the sister.

"Excuse me, I've convinced your sister to let the children stay here for a few more days. If you do what my partner told you to do, then you shouldn't have anymore problems."

"Oh thank you officer. I'm surprised she listened to you. She usually hates the police."

Back at the car, my partner curiously said, "She was so set on leaving with those kids. What did you say to her to get her to change her mind?"

"It's a Black thang partner. If I told you, you wouldn't understand," I replied.

"What's this Black thing you guys are always talking about and why can't us White people understand it?" she asked with excitement.

I just laughed. I didn't tell her what I did because I didn't trust her. If the situation would have been reversed, there was good chance that I would have told on her, especially in court. Also, I didn't want her to think that it was okay for her to do the same. This was a once in a lifetime occurrence for me. I swore I'd never lose my cool or let my personal feelings dictate my actions again. My promise would soon be broken.

Although my partner was always willing and eager to catch a bad guy, a couple of times she just plain screwed up. One night we received a robbery call at the Pizza Hut

97

restaurant on 43rd St. and Leimert Blvd. We were advised the suspect used a handgun to rob the place and then fled the scene on a bicycle with thirty dollars in currency. My partner and I were responding to the call from the far end of the division in rush hour traffic. It took us approximately thirty minutes to get to our destination.

"This idiot will be long gone by the time we get there," my partner said.

"All we have to do is take the report. You think they'll give us a couple of slices of pizza when we're done?"

"I doubt it. They're not that friendly to the police."

"That's why they got robbed!"

We stopped at a red light one block away from the Pizza Hut. Suddenly, I saw a young man on a bicycle ride up to the front door of the restaurant. The young man exited his bicycle. He then reached under his shirt and pulled out a handgun.

"Am I seeing things or is our robbery suspect robbing the same place twice?"

"I can't believe it! The moron didn't get enough money the first time so he came back for more," she shouted.

My partner floored the car and sped through the red light. The suspect looked at us, tucked his weapon down in his pants and climbed back on his bicycle. The robber then peddled as fast as he could but he couldn't out run the patrol car. In the middle of the chase, he briefly took his eyes off his path and looked back at the fast closing patrol car. Before he could turn back around, he crashed into a tree and fell head first onto the pavement. I popped out of the patrol car and quickly handcuffed the robber.

98

"Let me search him."

"That's okay, I got it," I responded.

"No, I'll do it," she insisted.

I then handed the handcuffed suspect over to my partner for the search. My partner proceeded to run her hands over the robber's clothing. After she concluded her search she led the suspect to the back door of the police car and sat him inside.

"Did you find the gun?" I asked her.

"No, there wasn't any gun."

"Yes there was. I saw one."

"I didn't see one and I didn't find one on him so there must not have been one," she sarcastically answered.

"He must have tossed it somewhere."

We then called more units to our location. We mapped out the suspect's escape route and gave officers instructions to search the area and find the missing weapon. About a dozen officers searched under cars and in bushes for the handgun. Twenty minutes later, I returned to the patrol car to get my flashlight.

"What are you guys looking for?" the suspect asked me.

"The gun," I replied.

"What gun?"

"The gun you tossed on us!"

"I didn't toss a gun officer."

I became irritated. "Look, don't lie! I saw you with a gun."

"I know officer but I didn't throw it."

"What did you do with it then?" I asked.

99

"It's in my pants pocket. I thought your partner felt it."

I reached inside the suspect's pocket and recovered the weapon. "Thanks sir for telling me. I appreciate it," I told him. I then motioned for my partner to come over to the car. "Oh partner, can you come here for a moment dear?"

I then told her of my findings. Of course she refused to believe me so I solicited the help of the suspect. "Where was the gun?" I asked.

"In my pocket," the suspect answered.

My partner was crushed. I felt sorry for her even though she jeopardized our safety. I knew that she could be suspended if a sergeant found out. Nobody wanted to work with her as it was. If the other male officers had found out, they would have really objected to working with her. On my partner's behalf, I notified the other officers that I had found the missing weapon underneath a parked car.

A sergeant approached me and asked, "Which car did you find the gun under?"

I pointed to a red Ford Mustang and replied, "That one sir."

"That's weird, I looked under that one and didn't see anything."

"It was way under there and jammed under the front wheel," I answered.

Two months later on a Wednesday, my partner's name was on the transfer list to a valley division.

"Why are you leaving Southwest Division?" I asked her.

"I have to get out of the south end because everybody that I come in contact with is either a gang member, a base

100

head, or a derelict. I've got to leave South Central LA before I start hating all Black people and Mexicans."

Her comments aroused my curiosity. She was a college graduate yet she was not able to understand that police officers basically only deal with the dregs of society. Surely, any intelligent person would not come to a conclusion of a whole race based on a few. Her comment made me wonder if she was not trying to suppress those feelings all along.

STRESSING!

"Westwood (community near UCLA. campus) is gone. The Blacks have discovered it."

Former LAPD Detective Mark Fuhrman. (Based on transcripts used by the O.J Simpson defense lawyers)

When I was a sprouting teenager, my buddies and I would pile four deep into my mother's red 1981 Chevy Monte Carlo and cruise down Crenshaw Blvd. looking for girls. What else was a young Black teenager to do on the weekends? There weren't enough good movies in the theaters to spark our interest on a regular basis. If there had been more movies that attracted young Black teenage audiences, my friends and I wouldn't have been able to afford to go every weekend anyway. As an alternative, we would put on *def* clothes and try to get our *mack* on while cruising "The Shaw."

On Sunday night I would be included among thousands of teenagers and young adults who cruised up and down a three-mile stretch of Crenshaw Blvd. between Adams Blvd. and Manchester Ave. It was not uncommon to see both sides of the Boulevard jammed packed with low-rider cars and herds of young men and women. Most of the youths joyfully gathered around and talked with the hopes of exchanging phone numbers. Ninety-eight percent of the young people were polite, respectful, and well behaved.

Unfortunately, two percent of those who cruised the Boulevard were savage and hostile gang

102

members. Sometimes they drove as far as three hundred miles from Las Vegas in stolen cars. Sadly, some of the gang members cruised Crenshaw Blvd. to meet girls and shoot rival gang members or whichever came first. The majority of the shooting victims who lay in the middle of the police crime scene tape were innocent non-gang affiliated bystanders who were cruelly gunned down while trying to have fun just as I was.

Surprisingly, ten years later, my new partner and I still cruised "The Shaw." Things had definitely changed. In my day young men sported designer haircuts with numerous parts carved in them. Fresh Fila sweat suits and K-Swiss tennis shoes were the preferred attire. In the present day too many young men choose to wear Pendleton shirts, baggy clothing or sagging khaki pants with a red or blue rag hanging out of their back pocket.

The appearances of teenagers weren't the only things that had changed. Over the course of ten years my partner and I had also taken on a new look. We were no longer cruising the Boulevard looking for girls in our parent's cars. Now we were in a black and white police car looking for gang members. As a patrol officer for the LAPD, our primary objective was to maintain law and order in the Crenshaw District. Every Sunday night we would volunteer to work the Crenshaw Blvd. cruiser task force. It felt good to finally work with someone who shared some of my same interests.

My new partner was a young Black brother about my age who grew up in the Nickerson Garden Projects. When he was eleven years old, his father moved his family out of Watts and into the Valley. My partner spoke English so properly that White officers teased him.

103

"You're a White man trapped inside of a Black man's body!"

I had my doubts at first but I learned not to judge a book by its cover. After all these same officers said I was a crip trapped in a LAPD uniform. That was far from the truth.

Usually the first couple weeks of summer were hectic and often dangerous on *The Shaw*. On Sunday nights, the three-mile area averaged one shooting, one carjacking, and one robbery every half-hour from sundown until 2:00 a.m. At the beginning of summer, LAPD arrested so many people with guns, the captain of the division and the City Council person for the district were forced to close down the street from 6:00 p.m. until midnight.

Despite LAPD's efforts teenagers still cruised on Sunday nights but not as freely. If anyone had the appearance of a rough neck, they usually got pulled over without officers pondering probable cause. It was not uncommon to see LAPD officers *jacking-up* young Black teenagers along the Boulevard. Patrol officers often unintentionally pulled over some good kids thinking they were gang members. At first this scene bothered me but then I painfully learned to accept it as a community ritual. Officers tried to rationalize their actions by saying, "I'd rather apologize to someone for stopping them than apologize to a mother for not preventing her child from being killed." Some officers were sincere, others weren't.

One Sunday night, my partner and I brought a big portable cassette player to work. All night long, we drove up and down the Boulevard and listened to Ice Cube sing, "Nobody I knew got killed in South Central LA. Today was a

104

good day." *Damn, it's hard to believe that we are still cruising on Crenshaw Blvd*, I thought.

"Remember when we were young? We use to cruise down Crenshaw on Sunday nights and around Westwood Village on Friday and Saturday nights," I added.

"Yep, and then the gangs started shooting each other and messed it up for everyone!"

"Eventually they screw up every free teenage social event."

"Yep, and then everybody wants to get mad at the police for closing down the streets."

"Now you've got me pissed off," I said. "Let's pull over some gang members and violate their rights. Let's make them pay by taking their cars."

A training officer once told me that because gang members were immune to jail, the only way to make them hurt was to impound their cars or date their women. Impounding their cars was enough for me. The second was only a thought, although *cock blocking* was just as good. Without looking very hard we spotted four hard heads parked in a no parking zone on Crenshaw Blvd. The hard heads were standing outside of their low-rider talking to some females. My partner quickly made a U-turn and pulled up next to the group.
"Excuse me fellas but you guys have to get in your car and leave," my partner politely stated.

"Why, we ain't doing nothin but talkin to some womens," one smartly said.

"Can you read?" I asked.

"Yeah, I can read, can you?"

105

"If you can read then why are you parking underneath a no parking sign?"

None of the four hard heads made any attempt to walk back to their car. Instead they turned back around and continued talking to the females.

Opening the car door I angrily yelled, "Don't make me get out the car and hurt you!"

As soon as they heard the door open, they scurried back into the low-rider.

One asked, "Can I just get this honey's number before we go?"

"Hell no!" I shouted. "If you want a number I'll give you a number, a booking number!"

The guys then sped away and the women rushed toward their car.

"Don't worry officer, we leaving," one woman said.

"I said they had to leave, not you! Come on over here girl and talk to *da* police," I replied.

"What we look like talking to *da* police? Ain't you suppose to be workin or somethin?"

"I am. I'm protecting and serving. Can't you tell?"

One of the ladies lowered her head and took a look inside of the patrol car. Focusing her attention on me, she said, "You *kinda* cute. You can protect and serve me anytime!"

Turning toward my partner I whispered, "Which one do you want?"

"Whichever one you don't want," he answered.

"I'll take the dark one with the gold extensions in her hair and the long nails."

106

"You mean the one with all that junk in her trunk?" he asked.

"Yeah, that one. The one with the ghetto booty!"

When we were not working the cruiser detail, we were taking care of the usual business. My partner was quickly becoming stressed out from all of the verbal harassment we were getting from the Southwest citizens. After the completion of almost every call, my partner would clinch both fists in frustration and scream.

"Man! I can't take this anymore. I've got to get the hell out of LA!"

At first I thought that it was funny. "Aw, listen to him. He's cursing. How cute," I'd say.

Profanity didn't sound right coming from his mouth but the more he said it, the more I became concerned. I tried to console my partner by reminding him the attacks on him were not personal but an out lash of their frustrations with the judicial system.

"Take it from me, if they saw you off-duty they wouldn't give you a second look."

My effort to calm my partner didn't work as he continued to stress out with each call. One time, we were standing in the parking lot of a 7-Eleven convenience store drinking coffee in between calls. Suddenly, our break time was interrupted by a radio call.

"Three Adam Fifteen, Three Adam Fifteen handle a screaming woman call at 2701 S. Manhattan Pl. A woman is heard screaming for help in apartment number five," a female voice broadcasted.

107

Picking up my radio, I replied, "Three Adam Fifteen roger!"

"Three Adam Fifteen handle code three."

Dropping our coffee cups we ran to the patrol car and sped out of the parking lot with our lights and siren activated. Before jetting through an intersection I looked to my right and yelled, "Clear right" "Clear right" meant there was no opposing traffic and "Traffic" meant there was.

"Oh boy! It's gonna be one of those nights. Watch this be a robbery, kidnap, and rape in progress. This is going to be an all night caper. I just know it is!"

"Naw, it's just *gonna* be some chick having an orgasm, probably by herself."

Actually, we had no idea what to expect. At the time, this particular street was known for heavy drug trafficking and sales. There had been a number of drug related shootings and homicides on this street in the past years. The call could have been anything.

Several blocks from the address of the call my partner killed the lights, siren, and, headlights. In stealth mode the black and white cruised up to the apartment complex. The first thing I noticed was that all of the regular street corner drug dealers were absent. This meant they were either somehow involved with our call or for some reason they knew we were coming. Either way meant trouble.

Quietly creeping up to the apartment window my partner looked inside to see what was happening. Through the window he saw a young woman tied up in a chair. As she quietly sobbed an irate man held a hatchet and paced the floor around her.

108

"I know you sleeping with another man! Who is he? Who is he?" the man yelled.

"No one! I'm not sleeping with no one but you!"

"Don't lie to me you whore!"

The man then knelt down and removed one of the woman's shoes. "I'm gonna chop off your toes one by one until you tell me who you are sleeping with!"

My partner having seen enough concluded the woman was in serious danger. Looking over at me and whispered, "There's a woman tied up inside. The suspect has a hatchet in his hand and he's about to chop off her toes. Move in now! Go! Go!"

I was willing and more than ready to kick down the front door but I thought it would be wise to turn the door knob first to see if the door was unlocked. Quietly turning the doorknob I placed my shoulder against the door and pushed. I wasn't surprised when the door opened. It's not uncommon for suspects to get so involved in what they are doing they leave the front door unlocked or wide open. My push caused the wooden door to swing open with such force it slammed back into the wall. The impact shook the house and made a loud booming noise.

"Don't move a muscle!"

The armed suspect looked stunned as he looked back and saw two guns pointing in his face. His eyes widened and his mouth froze open.

"Drop the knife or you're dead! I'd love to blow you away!"

Without another word being said the suspect dropped the hatchet. I then rushed over to the man and handcuffed

109

him. The man looked puzzled. His eyes were still bucked as he wildly looked around the room in disbelief.

"What's going on? You guys can't come in here like this! Do you have a search warrant?"

"Shut up! We don't need a warrant. You've been watching too much television."

My partner walked over to the woman who also looked bewildered by our arrival. Whipping out a pocketknife, my partner carefully sliced off the ropes restraining the woman.

"Do you know this guy ma'am?"

"He's my boyfriend. We've only been dating for three months and he's crazy!"

"Has he done this before?"

"No, he's usually a real sweet guy but he's real jealous."

Pulling out a 1x3 inch field interview card he asked, "What's his name?"

"Everton something, I don't know his last name."

"Where does he live?"

"I don't know. Most of the time he stays here."

Taking a deep breath, my partner's face displayed a look of disgust. "Wait just a dog-gone minute here lady! You mean to tell me that you've been dating someone for three months and you don't know his last name or where he lives? Give me a break! Lady, do I look like I was born yesterday?"

The victim just casually shrugged her shoulders signaling she had no explanation. My partner shook his head and walked over to the other side of the room where I was attempting to interview the uncooperative suspect.

Grabbing onto the handcuffs I lead the suspect out of the apartment and to the patrol car. The same street that was empty just minutes ago was now filled with curious spectators. People were standing on balconies, leaning out of windows and jamming the sidewalk near the patrol car. To please the on-looking crowd, I opened the back door of the car and gently helped the suspect inside. Once we were inside the patrol car and driving off I again attempted to interview him.

"What's your name sir?" I asked.

"None of your business! What's your name?"

"Let's not make this difficult. What's your name sir?" I asked again.

"What are you arresting me for? I didn't do nothing!"

"Well, I guess if you call trying to chop off your girlfriend's toes nothing then I guess you're being arrested for nothing."

"I wasn't going to chop her toes off. I was only playing. She knows that," he said.

"How come you can't play cards, dominoes or Scrabble like most people? What about Monopoly? I bet you use to play chop the toes off the donkey when you were a kid, huh?" I laughed.

"You know what? I don't like you. You think this is funny. You enjoy taking Black people to jail don't you? You're not a real Black man."

Interrupting him, I finished off his sentence by saying, "you're an Uncle Tom! I know! I know!"

The suspect's remark infuriated my partner. "What did you say?"

111

Not backing down, he repeated, "You're an Uncle Tom! I'm not afraid of you!"

"Hey partner!" I said. "I think the butcher needs an attitude adjustment before we get to the station."

"Which alley do you want? How about the one on 27th St. and Western Ave?"

"Not that one. That's the one where we almost got busted for putting that gang member's eye out. He also had an attitude."

The suspect's look of cockiness gave way to an expression of terror. The Rodney beating accompanied by many other truthful stories about LAPD beating people in dark alleys brought fear to almost everyone. Even though I didn't condone beatings or have any intentions of carrying out the threat, I didn't have a problem using LAPD's bad reputation to my advantage.

"What are you going to do, take me in an alley and beat me like Rodney King?"

"I don't think he was beaten in an alley. He was beaten on a public street and you see what mess that caused. Besides, he was beaten by two White guys. You're going to get an Afro-American beating."

"Yeah, you're not going to get a beating, you're gonna get beat down!"

Spotting an alley, my partner slowed the car and asked, "How's this?"

"Too bright!"

"How can two brothers beat up on another brother?" he asked.

112

"Oh, so now we're brothers? A minute ago we weren't Black men. A minute ago we were Uncle Toms!"

"My brotha." the suspect said. "My last name is Hope. My birth date is April 9, 1965. What else do you want to know?"

"I want you to apologize for calling us Uncle Toms. You hurt my feelings. When my feelings get hurt I have to hurt back," I told him.

"I'm sorry officers. You're not Uncle Toms. You're just doing your jobs."

"Aw," my partner whined. "Does this mean we're not going to beat um?"

"Roger! To the station," I responded.

The suspect looked relieved. When we arrived at the station, we immediately placed him in the holding tank and closed the door.

"You know what?" the suspect shouted through the door.

"What?" I asked.

"You're still an Uncle Tom and a sell out!" he shouted.

This episode of course added to my partner's woes. He just couldn't take the abuse any longer. It was only a matter of time before he'd snap and maybe unintentionally hurt someone.

One thing that made Southwest Division more interesting than other divisions was that it bordered five other divisions and parts of the county area. Whenever the bordering divisions became extremely busy, units were borrowed from Southwest to fill the void.

113

One night, all of the 77th units and Southeast units were tied up on several homicide scenes. My partner and I received a call in Watts. As we drove through the entrance of the Nickerson Gardens Projects, I reminded my partner that at the time, Southeast Division's policy was to send at least two units to every call inside the projects in fear of an ambush. I also reminded him there wasn't anyone available to back us up if anything went wrong. My partner shook like a leaf.

After completing our call, I persuaded him to drive through the projects and see if he could remember where he once lived.

Terrified, he said, "My father made a lot of sacrifices so that he could move me out of here before I got killed. Now you want me to throw it all away and get shot for nothing."

As we slowly drove through the projects, my partner began reminiscing about his childhood experiences. Pointing to different apartments, he yelled in excitement.

"Miss Ann use to live there! My friend Tommy and I use to play over there everyday! My father..."

Just then, six insane looking Grape Street crips wearing all purple clothing stepped in front of the patrol car. Everyone who has ever lived in South Central LA or Watts has heard of the Grape St. crips. Their reputation goes back to the beginning of gang existence.

"Oh Gosh! I'm running them over!" my partner said.

"Relax man. Let's see what they want," I said as I opened the door to get out of the car.

"You go ahead. I'll wait here for you."

As I stepped out of the car, I asked, "Who are you guys, the California raisins?"

114

"What are you doing in here by yourself? We only let a few One Time come in here at night by themselves! The others get blasted on," he said with hostility. He then shouted, "Pookie, go get the gauge (shotgun). We gon blast these fools!"

As he ordered, one of his boys took off in a full sprint and disappeared between the projects.

"I know most of the One Time from the station on 108th St. and Main. Ya'll don't look familiar," he said.

"We're from Southwest Division," I replied.

"I been there be-fo. What ya'll doing up in here?"

"My partner grew up over here. We came back to see if he still knew anybody."

The gang member ducked down and looked into the window of the patrol car and asked, "Why is your partner sitting in the car sweating by himself with the engine on and all the windows rolled up?"

"He's got the flu." I told him.

"Yeah, there's a lot of that going around. I had it last week. Tell that fool to drink a lot of liquids. Soup is good fo that too."

Tapping on the window I motioned for my partner to come out of the car. With great hesitation he did. The gang members greeted him with a handshake as if they were old friends. They seemed happy and intrigued to meet someone who had escaped the horrors of the projects and became a police officer. Within a short time my partner and the fellas were name-dropping all the people they knew in their age range. Shockingly nine of the eleven childhood playmates my partner mentioned were deceased.

115

"Damn, if you wouldn't have left out of here you would probably be dead too," one said.

The conversation was cut short by a radio call. We shook hands and drove off. It was probably a good thing we left when we did because a growing number of people were standing in the distance shouting, "Kill *da* police!"

As we exited the projects, I asked my partner, "Do you plan on transferring to Southeast Division so you can help out your old community?"

"Hell no! I'm getting out of LA! You should leave too. I don't understand how you can live around the corner from thugs, shop at grocery stores that have to close at midnight and listen to sirens and police helicopters all night. I'm tired of all this crap. I'm getting the heck out!"

My partner was not the only Black officer whom I'd seen get mentally twisted by the effects of the streets. The LA riot was a true test of character for all Afro-American police officers. During the 1992 LA riot, I witnessed two of my Black partners display hostility toward South Central LA citizens.

During the 1992 riot, the inside of the police station was just as chaotic as the streets. Officers were wandering around the station aimlessly waiting for instructions. Eventually, I was teamed up with a young, Black female officer who had about the same amount of time on the job as I had. Without clear instructions, we were thrown to the wolves. Our instructions were vague. There was a major riot occurring but officers were told not to get involved in anything major. We were ordered to stay available in case the fire department needed assistance.

116

Like a bad nightmare I went from comfortably sitting in the police station to the burning depths of hell. It was as if I had stepped through the television set and into the twilight zone. The streets of LA were chaotic. Everything was on fire. Through the smoke I saw hundreds of people running around taking whatever they pleased. As my partner and I drove on the lawless streets, I feared the unexpected. I had no idea what to expect from the looters or angry citizens. Unsnapping my holster I removed my gun and wedged it between my thighs.

Ironically, our first call was at the Boys Market on Western Ave and Jefferson Blvd. To me this wasn't just any supermarket. This was the market where I as a community resident shopped. From a distance it didn't appear anything major was happening inside of the market. Carefully surveying the premises I noticed there were only two cars parked in the parking lot. Then I noticed the front glass door of the market was broken but I couldn't see anyone inside. We slowly drove into the parking lot and turned on our lights and siren.

Like roaches running when the lights come on, about sixty people came stampeding out of the broken glass door. Picking up the P.A., I ordered everyone to immediately exit the store. Of course we had no intention of arresting anyone as ordered. We only wanted to clear everyone out of the market.

The last people to leave the store were an overweight woman in her mid sixties accompanied by two children around seven years old. The woman was carrying a smoked ham while the children were carrying an arm full of dolls and plastic toys. Gingerly stepping through the broken glass door, the

117

woman lost her balance and then slipped and fell face down in a sea of broken glass. The children looked back and continued running out of the parking lot carrying their new toys. Crying and covered with blood grandma reached out her hand and pleaded.

"Please help me. I'm hurt."

I looked at my partner who was laughing. "Do you think we should help her?" I asked with great concern.

"Hell no!" she angrily answered. "She got exactly what she deserved. She shouldn't be out here looting with her grandchildren. That's a damn shame!"

"I have to do something," I said. "That could be my mother lying down there."

"Is your mamma out here looting?" she asked.

"No."

"Okay then. Let's get out of here. I'm hungry." I concluded. "Hold on."

I felt compelled to do something. Slipping on a pair of latex gloves, I crunched through the fallen glass and helped the woman to her feet. The woman hobbled a few steps and then bent down in an attempt to pick the smoked ham up from the ground.

"Don't even think about it!" my partner yelled.

Disappointed, grandma straightened up and gave us a dirty look before limping out of the parking lot empty handed.

"Did you see that?" my partner asked. "Black people are always trying to take advantage of one another. I bet she wouldn't have done that if we had been White. If we had been two White boys she probably would have gotten her fat butt kicked and maybe even arrested. That's why I'm taking my

118

Black self out of this division and to the Valley. I'm sick of this crap. What's wrong with your people?"

"My people? They're your people too!" I responded.

"Not anymore. I've given up on Black people, at least these ignorant fools down here!"

It was weird hearing her say that. I wondered how many other Black officers felt the way she did about South Central citizens. I then wondered if one day the job would cause me to denounce my race as she did.

"Everybody that lives down here is not ignorant. We just only come across those that are," I said.

I was leery about participating in the conversation because I had been burned once before for giving my honest opinion on racial issues. Even though I knew the consequences I couldn't resist the temptation.

"Let me ask you something. Is it just me or do you find that when you ask a victim a question, nine out ten times they turn towards your White partner and answer it?" I asked.

"Oh hell yeah!" my partner replied. "Asians really have that bad. They feel like a Black police officer doesn't know what they're talking about."

Before I became a police officer, I refused to patronize foreign businesses because I was always being treated rudely as if they were doing me a favor by letting me spend my money in their store. They begged me to come into their stores when I was on-duty. They pleaded with me to stay and eat their stale, old, outdated food.

When I was a teenager my friends and I would ride our bicycles down to the neighborhood liquor store to buy sodas. Like most liquor stores around my neighborhood this

119

liquor store was owned and operated by Asian Americans. Every time I walked into the store, an employee would closely follow me around the store to make sure I did not steal anything. This made me feel very uncomfortable. In order to get the employee to back off, I had to over exaggerate my desire to make a purchase. It was as if I had to walk into the store, hold up my money and shout, "It's okay. I'm going to buy something."

One day a Mexican man carrying a picket sign in front of the liquor store stopped me.

"Hey little amigo. We are picketing this store because they refuse to hire anyone but their own race. Please do not buy anything from here until they hire a minority," he pleaded.

I immediately turned around and went home. From that day on I never again set foot in another liquor store that only employed one race until I became a police officer.

"Even now if I walk into an Asian owned and operated convenient store to handle a radio call, I still feel like I'm being watched!" I added.

What really bothered me was that I knew there were a lot of people who wore Korean made Malcolm X paraphernalia and had no idea what it represented. Even the merchants who sold the merchandise had no idea what the "X" meant. One time, I went to a call at the La Brea Swap Meet. Some Korean merchant who was selling Malcolm X T-shirts came up to me.

"You want to buy shirt? Ten dolla," she said with a heavy accent.

I was curious to see if she knew what the X meant. "What's the X on that shirt mean?" I asked.

"That's X. X is a letter. Brack people love letter X. That's Brack peoples' favorite letter. You like X?" she responded.

At first, I felt like kicking over her stand and running out of the Swap Meet with her T-shirts but I was on-duty and in uniform. Then I realized I couldn't fault her for making money off other's ignorance. I also realized the people who bought her shirts were the same people who called me a sellout.

MY PARTNER AND I SUDDENLY RECEIVED A BACK-UP REQUEST from the fire department at Adams Blvd. and Harvard Blvd. Earlier in the evening a fire fighter had been shot in the face while trying to put out a fire. Our primary objective was to back up the fire department. Unfortunately, we had to let the looters have the market.

When my partner and I arrived at the scene, there were about seventy angry people standing in the street throwing rocks and bottles at fire fighters who were attempting to extinguish an upholstery store blaze.

Dressed in riot gear along with twenty-five other officers, we formed a skirmish line. With our batons drawn we marched down toward the hostile crowd. Just as it was about to become *hammer time*, thirty members from the First A.M.E. church stepped in front of the squad. The members joined hands and formed a human chain between the officers and the crowd. Their intentions were to stop the officers from beating up on what they thought were innocent bystanders. I didn't mind the human chain because the church congregation acted as a shield and kept me from being hit by bottles. Besides I could empathize with them. They felt there was no justice. If

121

there was justice, most of the hostile crowd would have still been behind bars. Deep down I really didn't feel like beating anyone. My mind was still in shock, not only from the frenzy but also at the loss of my days off.

Several minutes after the congregation's sudden arrival one of their leaders was hit in the head by a bottle and knocked unconscious. This caused the congregation to disappear as quickly as they came.

Once again the angry officers began to march on the hostile crowd. As we advanced, a man stood in front of me and said, "Hey brother, lay down your weapons and come join us."

I could use a wide screen TV and a set of new tires for my car.

The sergeant in charge stopped the officer's offensive assault just a few feet short of the crowd. For an hour, fifty LAPD officers dressed in riot gear stood by and dodged rocks and bottles like punks. During the whole time I had to listen to my own Black brothers and sisters single out the few Black officers who were there. They relentlessly called us names like, Uncle Tom, sell outs and fake Black men.

Serious questions cluttered my thoughts. *Why were the Black officers being singled out? None of them had ever beaten anyone with a baton. Why were the Black officers sellouts for working in the Black community? Most of us went through a lot of hardship to get there.*

"Uncle Tom, sellout," echoed continuously in my ears. Those words slowly chipped at my outer armor. I was then stabbed directly in the heart when my integrity as a Black man was questioned. "You're not a real Black man!" the crowd shouted. "If you were, you'd be with us!"

My views changed drastically within that hour. I was now ready to beat down anyone who came in arms reach.

If they don't care about me then I ain't gonna give them a second thought!

Fortunately for everyone, the fire was soon extinguished and the officers left the scene.

The next call we responded to was a drive-by shooting near Jefferson Blvd. and Buckingham Rd. As we cautiously approached the location, we could see a small crowd of people standing in the middle of the street. As my partner and I got closer, we saw several people standing around a sprawled out body.

Several members of the crowd spotted the Black and White and began waving frantically for the unit to hurry up. I carefully scanned the street for snipers as my partner slowly inched the patrol car toward the victim and the crowd. Being ever so cautious I looked behind cars, around bushes, in trees, on roofs, and anywhere I thought a person could lay in wait to ambush us. The downed victim was secondary. My partner's and my life came first.

Thick bright red blood curdled from a penny size hole in the victim's chest. While I surveyed the damage, my partner requested a paramedic to respond code 3. I was not a medical expert but in my opinion the twenty-year-old gang member's chances of survival did not look good. Normally, when officers think a person isn't going to make it they immediately secure the crime scene with yellow crime scene tape. Then, they will usually start interviewing potential witnesses but because of

123

the citywide riot, my partner and I were going to do a *fast food* homicide investigation. If the gang member died, we were going to have the paramedics scoop him up and dump him off at the nearest hospital until detectives could do an investigation after the riot was over. We weren't about to interview any hostile people.

Several minutes after we requested a paramedic we were informed by the fire department that they wouldn't leave the fire station without a police escort. They didn't care if someone was dying. Like the police their safety was a priority. My partner radioed another unit and asked them to respond to the fire station and escort the fire department ten blocks from their station to the victim's location. That took another fifteen minutes. Eventually, the fire department arrived and transported the victim to a hospital. I have no idea if he survived because a report was not taken.

Today the Los Angeles City Fire Department still has a similar policy to the one they used during the riot. Most of the fire fighters who work in South Central LA wear bulletproof vests underneath their uniforms. Also, they will not respond to a shooting or a stabbing call until the police have arrived and declared the scene safe. Many officers have literally seen gang members bleed to death because their homies refused to leave their side as requested by a police officer.

After the paramedics transported the victim to the hospital my partner and I continued to follow the fire department from fire to fire all night long. Most of the fires we responded to had been extinguished earlier in the evening but because of the volume of fires in the city, the fire department wasn't able to do a thorough job. Fires continued to flare back up throughout the night.

The second night of the riot was not as chaotic as the first. Probably because there wasn't much left to steal. The additional ten thousand police officers and federal agents from all over the nation helped. LAPD was now impressively rolling four deep to a car, not because of safety reasons but because the department was short on cars and radios. Every other car on the street was a police car. Although the looting was down, fires continued to burn out of control.

I had two federal agents and a fifteen-year LAPD veteran in my car. The fifteen-year veteran was a thick, dark colored Black man in his late thirties. He had a bushy mustache that resembled a walrus. He was infamous for his bad attitude and quick temper. In looking at him I could see a projection of myself. Like myself the veteran was extremely confident and he didn't take mess from anyone.

Looking out the window in a hypnotic stare the fifteen-year veteran said, "This reminds me of Da Nang in 1968. It was crazy just like this."

Interrupting him I said, "You're not going to have a Rambo flashback are you?"

His nervousness turned into hostility. "I'm not afraid! You're too stupid to understand!"

"Relax dude! Just cause you're afraid, don't take it out on me!" I joked.

"All you young officers think that you're 'the man' by chasing your tails after people but you're not doing anything. While you were in diapers wondering where you were going to get your milk from, I was fighting V.C's in Nam."

125

"Oh no! Not a Vietnam story!"

"You ain't nothing! You ain't nothing. This is just like Nam!"

Suddenly, I was more afraid of my partner than I was of what was going on around me. I feared my partner was going to start screaming, "In coming" and then start shooting out the window.

"Can I ask you something? Are you on drugs?" I asked my partner.

"Let me out the car!"

"Relax. I'm on your side," I told him

There was nothing else for me to do so I jokingly messed with my stressed out partner all night long. My partner swore never to work with me again and to this day he hasn't.

For the next three weeks I worked at least twelve hours a day, seven days a week. Everyone in the department was physically and mentally drained. Tempers were short. Every night officers had to be separated from fighting one another. It was really an unforgettable time for Afro-American police officers. Comments like, "If these people want to burn and loot their own neighborhood then let them do it" and "As long as they stay out of my neighborhood let them loot," troubled many Black officers.

After the riot I was watching the news and was surprised to learn that a young man whom I graduated from high school with, Henry Watson, was arrested for taking part in the Reginald Denny beating. An aerial videotape filmed by a news helicopter captured the young man placing his foot on the back of Reginald Denny's neck after he was pulled out of his truck. Watson's actions were similar to that of Officer Ted

126

Brisenio during the Rodney King beating. My schoolmate was subsequently arrested and charged with attempted murder.

In my opinion, the District Attorney was really reaching for straws and overcharging Watson. There was no way a jury was going to convict him of attempted murder for placing his foot on someone's neck. That was a misdemeanor battery at best.

Henry Watson and I almost played varsity football together during our senior year in high school. Unfortunately, I got mad at the coach and quit during the second day of practice. I felt since the coach heavily recruited me because of my speed, I should be exempt from his yelling. As I held myself up in push-up position, the coach stood over me and shouted, "If anyone on this team doesn't like the way I yell then they can leave!" Being a cocky teenager, I slowly stood up, brushed myself off, and walked out of practice.

I remembered the accused attacker as being a very nice person who politely spoke to everyone. I was shocked to see his picture on the news. That day I received about a dozen phone calls from former high school classmates who shared my sentiments. My schoolmate and I weren't close nor did I know much about his background, however he didn't appear to be prejudiced against White people. Sometimes I would see him walk home with White kids where he would have dinner with their families. Occasionally, I would see him trying to get his mack on to some of the White girls on campus. I couldn't help wonder if some of the anger he vented out on Reginald Denny wasn't caused by a flash back of a White girl calling him a racial slur. I knew the feeling from personal experience. Usually, whenever one of my White schoolmates became angry, the first words out of their mouth would be a racial slur.

Hmm? I wondered.

TROUBLE MAN

"Bangin' ain't no part-time thang, it's full-time, it's a career. It's bein' down when ain't nobody else down with you."

Los Angeles gang member "Monster" Kody Scott from his book: Monster, the Autobiography of an L.A. Gang Member. (1993)

Like my ex-partners I was beginning to be crushed by the weight of the job and the environment. Part of the problem was that I lived in the hood. While other officers went home and temporarily escaped, the horrors of the community still haunted me. During my second week out on patrol at Southwest, I fell in love with a house on one of the many quiet streets in the division. Two months later, I purchased it.

Unfortunately, my new dream home was right in the middle of the Harlem Rollin Thirties crips neighborhood. There were at least ten other gangs within a half-mile radius of my new home.

To the west I had the Black P-Stone bloods. Northwest of me was a West Blvd. crip neighborhood. Immediately south were Rolling Forty crips and Eighteenth Street. Northeast of my house there were the Rolling Twenty bloods, Fruit Town Brims, and Los Harpes. Within another half mile there had to be about thirty or more gangs. All of my friends and family said I must have been crazy to live in the same division as I worked. If I wasn't crazy then, I soon became crazy with paranoia.

I didn't sleep a wink the first night I moved. It seemed like the "ghetto bird" hovered over my house the entire night and shined its bright light through my window.

During the second week, a Datsun B210 came barreling down the street while I was outside watering my front lawn. The driver lost control of the car and crashed into a tree in front of my home. Three teenage boys around thirteen years old ran from the car and hid in some bushes directly across the street.

With the engine still running, I curiously took a look inside the car and saw it had been hot-wired. After turning the car off, I went inside my house and dialed 911. I told the operator someone was stealing a car in front of my house, which should have made the call high priority. In a sarcastic manner, the 911 operator asked me the same questions that I had asked others. The questions seemed stupid when I was asked.

"Three teenagers are stealing a car in front of my house," I said.

"How do you know the car is stolen sir?" the operator sarcastically asked.

"Because I am a police officer. That is how I know."

"Is it you car sir?" I was asked.

I took a deep breath and fought with all my strength not to call the operator *out of her name*.

Thirty minutes later, the police still had not arrived. The teenagers, figuring I had not phoned the police, returned to the car, re-hotwired it and drove off. Furious, I called the watch commander and demanded an explanation. I assumed the officers assigned to the call were probably sitting

130

at a convenience store drinking coffee and waiting for the suspects to leave so they wouldn't have to make an arrest.

According to the sergeant, the call was accidentally sent to another part of the city with a similar address. Based on personal experience I knew this was possible. The LAPD 911 system had so many flaws that a person could only hold their breath and pray for help.

I was speaking from experience. As a new officer, I was sentenced to work at Communications Division for a brief period. Communication Division was a fancy name for 911 operators. I had no ideal police officers along with civilians answered 911 calls. Imprisoned three stories beneath City Hall without windows, days of bitterness elapsed.

I was forced to hang up my gun and handcuffs in exchange for a pair of headsets. I was then reduced from a highly trained and physically fit fighting machine to a meager civilian employee. My ego was bruised. On the street I was an authority figure. At Communications Division I was nothing. I got no respect!

Ninety-five percent of the employees at Communications Division were women. Most of them despised police officers because they were either divorced from a cop or had been scorned in a dating relationship with one. The majority of them wouldn't speak to me even if I spoke first.

It was at Communications Division where I experienced the most frightening event of my life. Never before had I experienced sixty women menstruating at the same time. Sometimes they were so unruly that I felt as though I was sitting in the bleachers of an Oakland Raiders football game. Like clockwork, three to five days out of every month the women would scream, argue and almost come to blows with one another. They would end every argument by saying, "You'll have to excuse me, it's that time of the month." The other person involved would reply, "Girl, I know what you mean."

The few male employees who worked down there didn't care for police officers either. They thought police officers looked down on them for working as operators. They didn't speak either. The only people who showed me any attention were two gay employees. Eventually they stopped speaking when they found out I wasn't interested.

"Hey, we can still be friends. You can still say hi," I almost told them.

The division chain of command consisted of an LAPD captain, a couple of dysfunctional lieutenants and several sergeants who were field rejects. The lieutenant in charge of my watch was a tall dorky looking man with a Mexican surname. Rumor had it that ninety-nine percent of the time he considered himself Anglo. He would only admit to having Mexican decent on promotional exams. My lieutenant didn't have a clue as to what was going on in the division nor did he have any idea how it was operated. All of the supervisory decisions were left to senior civilian employees who governed the 911 control room like plantation overseers. They would pace the 911 floor to make sure the employees were constantly answering calls.

One long nightmare is how I would describe working at Communications Division. Located on every employee's 911 console was a small red light. The red light blinked continuously to the beat of a sixteenth note, indicating there were 911 calls on hold. The only time the light went off was when the 911 system wasn't holding calls. That damn light almost never stopped blinking. I would have nightmares involving that blinking light. Sometimes I would wake up screaming, "This is 911. What are you reporting?"

One particular call stays in mind. Once I received a call from a hysterical woman, which happened about every thirty seconds. "My brother got into an argument with my neighbor and my neighbor said he is going to get a gun and shoot him," the woman screamed into the phone.

Calmly, I replied, "Where is your neighbor now?"

"He went home to get a gun! Please hurry!"

"Is he White, Black or Hispanic?"

"Hurry, please hurry! Oh my God, here he is!" she screamed.

Pop! Pop! Pop!

Numerous gunshots sounded off through the phone and into my headset. The phone was then disconnected. *Damn, I guess she really did need the police*, I said to myself as I dispatched officers. *Oh well, next emergency call.*

MY ANGER WAS REPLACED WITH PARANOIA as I came to realize I was on my own as far as protection went. This incident clearly demonstrated that my comrades couldn't be counted on to assist me in a time of need. As a result, my four inch Smith And Wesson nine millimeter became an extension of my right hand.

I never went anywhere, including to the bathroom, without my gun. My worst fear was to have a carload of Rollin Thirty crips on their way to do a drive-by shooting, recognize

133

me while I was outside watering my yard and then open fire on me. My next biggest fear was to have someone kick in my front door while I was on the toilet and literally catch me with my pants down. I was so paranoid about this that I couldn't make a comfortable bowel movement without my gun resting at my feet. The thought of my coworkers standing over me laughing at my naked corpse was enough reason for me to be armed at all times.

I had stood in checkout lines behind gang members who swore to me while on duty, "Don't let me catch you out of that uniform! If I do, then it's on cuzz!"

Surprisingly, none of them ever gave me a second look. I then began to realize that most of the hostility I've experienced was not directed at me personally but to the man in uniform. If the threats were personal, surely someone would recognize me as their enemy. I can only think of three occasions when someone whom I've arrested recognized me and said something. All three encounters were friendly. Coincidentally, they all occurred while I was shopping at the Fox Hills Mall in Culver City.

One was a teenage girl whom I had arrested for being a passenger in a stolen car. The girl approached me as I was walking through the mall. Tapping me on the shoulder, she smiled and said, "Don't act like you don't know me, Mr. Police officer." The only reason I remembered her was because she was a sassy, loud mouth teenager, who I couldn't get to shut up.

"I'm surprised you recognized me out of uniform." I said.

"How could I ever forget the face of someone who made me lay face down in the middle of a crowded street? You made me mess up my good clothes. I've never been so embarrassed in my life."

"Sorry about that," I said. "The next time you steal a car, wear some old clothes."

"I didn't steal the car. My boyfriend did. He told me it was his aunt's."

We both joked about the incident and then went our separate ways. Another time, I was standing in line behind two gang bangers inside of the Foot Locker shoe store. One of the bangers glanced back at me and then did a double take. His eyes almost popped out of his head when he saw me.

"Aw man!" he screamed.

I immediately recognized him. For the past two weeks, I had been in court testifying against him on a robbery case. He failed to show up for court the day before sentencing. The judge issued a no bail felony warrant for his arrest.

Shaking, he nervously said, "I didn't show up to court the other day because my car broke down."

Interrupting him, I said, "Whatever." I really wasn't interested in hearing his excuse. I didn't get involved in crime prevention off-duty unless I was confronted with a life or death situation. The department rarely gave full support to officers who became involved in off-duty arrest. Somehow, the department always found a fault in officer's tactics, resulting in a suspension without pay.

Thirty seconds later the gangbanger stepped out of line and quickly walked out of the store. I assumed he turned himself in. I never bothered to check.

Coincidentally, the third incident also occurred inside of the Foot Locker shoe store. While making a sales pitch, my sales person stopped, snapped his fingers and said, "I know where I've seen you before. You probably don't remember me but you arrested me for carrying a gun about a year ago."

He was right. I didn't remember him. I had arrested many people for carrying guns. This time, I turned around and left the store.

As time went on, I noticed there were several locations where my chances of running into unfriendly people were higher than others. Taco Bell restaurant was one place. Every time I walked into a Taco Bell, I was sure to see someone whom I had arrested standing in line.

On warm days mothers peacefully pushed their babies around the neighborhood in strollers. There was no tranquility for me, not even on a warm day. My mind was so scarred by the nightly violence that I was always on alert.

Every street corner had a violent story; a girl was raped over there, a young boy gunned down right here, a man stabbed down there. For relaxation, on my off nights, I would sit on my front porch during the middle of the night and listen to the automatic gun fire echoing out in the night air. Trying to approximate its location, I'd wonder who was responsible. I would then wait a few minutes to see if I could hear sirens. If I could, then that indicated another victim had been claimed to the violent streets of LA. During the day I would sometimes

136

see women who were victims of spousal abuse shopping at the grocery store with their assailants affectionately by their side.

What's the use? Do I really make a difference or am I just punishing myself for caring?

A couple of times people have stopped me while on-duty and then began to question me as if I were their suspect.

"Why are you guys always messing with people?" I've been asked.

"Because that's what we are paid to do."

"Do you always carry your gun?"

"Always," I answered. "Sometimes I carry two."

"Why did you beat up Rodney King?"

"I didn't. I was off that night."

"Do you beat up on people?"

"Only on the weekends," I'd respond.

"I bet you do because you look mean. Do you ever smile?"

When I thought about it, it was true. I did look mean and I rarely smiled since becoming a police officer. Personal complaints, being shot at, punched, and having a gun jammed in my stomach weren't reasons to smile. I had literally stood over at least a half dozen young men, looked into their eyes, and helplessly watched the life slowly drain from their bodies. I can't even count how many times I've heard dying gang members say, "Please don't let me die officer."

There were many times when I had looked into the blank stare of a rape victim who was afraid to talk to me simply because I was a man. For some strange reason, Southwest Division had the highest amount of rapes in the city. Out of the multitudes of calls I had handled, the one that seemed to stick in my mind the most was one where a ten year old girl was abducted on a bus stop while on her way home from school. The suspect drove her to a vacant lot and raped her. After spitting and ejaculating on the victim, the man pulled out a Bible from underneath his seat and then read her scriptures from the book for an hour. Upon releasing the girl he told her, "You're no longer a virgin. You are a sinner. Get out!"

Sitting down and asking the ten year old questions like, "Was his penis erect?" and "Did he ejaculate?" was probably the most difficult task I had done since coming on the job because I felt awkward and helpless in that situation. No one ever heard that part of the job during LAPD recruitment advertisements. Twenty-eight years of growing up in Los Angeles had prepared me to deal with gang violence but there was nothing in the world that could have prepared me for handling a rape call.

I had given up hope. I was almost convinced I couldn't make a difference in my community. I basically didn't care anymore. I no longer cared about the job or people in general. Before becoming a police officer I took pride in the fact I didn't use profanity but now, the F word was part of my daily vocabulary. I must have said it at least ten times a day during radio calls.

I had become so detached and violent that I could have as easily beat down a fellow officer or sergeant as I would a criminal. On one occasion my partner and I responded to a drive-by shooting call. It was around 3:30A.M. Except for one dying gang member lying in the street, the neighborhood was quiet and deserted. After requesting a paramedic, we stood

138

over the dying victim who had been shot once in the eye and in the forehead.

"Aw man! Look, you can see his brain," my partner shouted.

While lying on his back, the nineteen-year-old blood gang member lifted up his blood soaked hand toward my partner. In a faint, blood gurgling voice he pleaded, "Please officer, hold my hand. I don't want to die alone. Hold my hand please."

"Hell no!" my partner responded. "You're bleeding too much." My partner then looked at me and asked, "How about you partner? Why don't you do it?"

It seemed almost sacrilegious to deny the dying man his last request. I truly felt sorry for the young man. For a brief moment, I actually thought about granting the dying man his last request. Unfortunately, for the victim, the patrol car was parked around the corner for tactical reasons and I was without latex gloves. My fear of getting a blood disease was far more a concern than making the gang member feel comfortable on his death bed.

"I'll have to pass," I answered.

"Please don't let me die alone!" the victim screamed as he began to tremble in shock.

"What's he doing partner?"

"I think he's going into shock," I replied.

My partner then extended his leg toward the victim's hand. "Here you go sir. You can hold my boot but don't touch my pants. If you get blood on my pants I'll kill you," he said with a grin.

"Thanks officer," the gang member answered.

He then weakly grabbed onto my partner's boot. We then curiously bent down over the victim and tried to re-count our high school biology and anatomy days.

"The blood on his head is thick and gooey. It's coagulating."

"Yep, and that yellow and white stuff is brain matter."

"You see how his eye popped out? That's from pressure applied to his skull."

"He's not going to make it partner, is he?"

"I don't think so!"

"Do you care?" I asked.

"Nope! Do you?" my partner responded.

"Yes."

Eventually I became more comfortable in my new neighborhood. I was still always strapped but I no longer feared walking to the corner market or eating at local fast food restaurants. If I did get recognized, so be it. I was no longer ducking and hiding from gang members whom I had stopped while on-duty.

Because of my odd working hours and unusual sleeping patterns, I hadn't spent any time with my family and friends. It was as hard as hell to convince a woman to let me come over at 3:00 a.m. To solve my social problem, I decided to throw an old fashion house party.

One Saturday evening, my friend Lowe and I crammed about one hundred and seventy-five people into my house and back yard for a party. About a dozen double-parked patrol cars lined the already crowded street. On-duty officers from all over the city ate and forcefully drank soft drinks until they received a radio call. The rest of the people partied nonstop until 3:00am.

The party was a social success. Several women found me interesting mainly because of my occupation, benefits and residence. Despite my good looks and charming personality, all the women I met soon dumped me. They all had the same complaint. I was cheap. The bad part of being a public servant was every woman in the city knew how much money I made and when I got paid. Every other Wednesday, my phone rang off the hook with women who wanted to see me. On the other days I was alone.

When I returned to work the next night, the watch commander told me he had received a call from the president of the Police Commission. The commissioner said one of my neighbors had phoned the station numerous times and asked for the party to be stopped. My neighbor saw twelve police cars parked out front of the house and wondered why nothing was being done about the loud music. I received a verbal warning for my actions.

DURING THE NEXT ROLL CALL, THE ATMOSPHERE WAS LOOSE. A fifteen-year veteran sergeant comfortably sat behind a desk in the front of the room. The large room was occupied with about thirty boisterous patrol officers. Every officer had their pencil and field officers' notebook in their hands. Everyone was anxiously waiting to jot down important information. Holding a large clipboard filled with papers, the sergeant began to read the notices and wanted information.

Speaking loudly, the sergeant announced, "Last night there was an officer involved shooting in the Rampart Division."

"Yeah! Let's hear it Serg. Brighten up our day," someone shouted.

"Last night at approximately 2300 hours, Officer Smith, twenty-six years old, serial number 27001 with five years on the job and officer Pete, thirty years old, serial number 26106, observed suspect John Franks walking northbound on 18th St. from Normandie Ave. Officers observed suspect with a gun. The suspect turned around and pointed the weapon at the officers. Officer Smith, fearing for his safety, fired sixteen rounds from his service nine millimeter Berretta and Officer Pete fired sixteen rounds from his weapon." Pausing from his reading, he asked, "Can anybody tell me why they fired sixteen rounds?"

"Because they only had sixteen rounds in their guns!" someone shouted.

Laughing, the sergeant replied, "You're absolutely right!"

"How many hits? The guy probably died of a heart attack from all the shooting."

"Let me finish! There's more. The suspect was fatally wounded and pronounced dead at the scene."

The roll call room erupted in joyful cheers and shouts. "Yeah!"   "Way to go!" "Yes, I love it!" "One less piece of crap to deal with!" "I love happy endings."

Regaining control, the sergeant yelled, "Hold it down! The next order of business is we have an extra patrol request at 1414 W. 36th St."

142

Interrupting the sergeant, someone yelled, "Don't tell me that there's a narcotics problem there!"

"Yes there is a narco problem there. Another thing, if you go to a domestic violence call, make sure you arrest the suspect if the situation calls for it. And don't forget to take a report to cover yourself."

An older officer got upset and shouted, "Forget these women! They want to be liberated but they also want us to give them special treatment when they get their butts kicked. If they don't want to press charges then we shouldn't do it for them. They always go back to their husbands anyway. That's stupid!"

The sergeant then told the officers a concerned citizen phoned the station and informed the desk officer there was going to be another drive-by shooting on 42nd St. and La Salle Ave. at midnight. 42nd St. and La Salle Ave. was right down the street from the police station. In two days, a total of two people were gunned down and killed, and four others were seriously injured. All this happened just one block away from the police station.

"A kind citizen phoned the station this morning and told the desk officer there is a rumor going around the neighborhood that there's going to be a drive-by shooting tonight at mid-night."

"So why doesn't this lady just tell her son not to do it!" an officer yelled out.

"Smiling, the sergeant said, "You know what that means, don't you? It means stay the hell away from that area! Wait until there's a dead body and then respond to set up a crime scene. That's all we are required to do."

143

Appalled by his remarks, I shouted, "What do you mean stay away from there! What in the hell are we here for?" I asked.

Another officer quickly spoke in the puzzled sergeant's defense. "Who cares about the gang members that live on that street? I hope they all get killed tonight. The last time there was a homicide on that street, they threw rocks and bottles at us and then they tried to make a personnel complaint against us when we pushed them away from the crime scene. On top of all that, we are working without a contract and the city doesn't want to give us a pay raise. I don't care what anybody says! I ain't doing nothing!"

"Everybody that lives on that street is not a gang member. There are a lot of good, hard working people that live there too. They need our help or else they wouldn't have called," I said.

"Why should we help them if they are afraid to help themselves. I bet the person who called didn't leave their name did they?"

"They never do," another added. "Even if we do arrest someone for a drive-by, no one is going to come forward and be a witness. It's a waste of time."

I spent the remaining forty minutes of roll call debating the whole watch as to why they should try and prevent a drive-by shooting on the same street as the station. Although I didn't agree with what the officers were saying, I did think their comments were somewhat warranted. Many times, police officers had almost been hurt in car accidents trying to get to radio calls quickly. Then once they apprehended the described suspect, the witness would refuse to identify him. The suspect

144

would subsequently be released and the officers would be criticized by the citizens for not doing anything.

That night, everyone except my partner and I obeyed the sergeant's orders to stay away from the battle zone. For hours we continuously drove up and down the street looking for drive-by shooters. The street was bare. There wasn't a gang member in sight for miles. I figured everyone was lying low until the threat of danger was over. Since nothing appeared to be going on, we decided to go one block up the street to use the restroom at the police station. As soon as we pulled into the station parking lot and got out of the patrol car, we heard rapid gunfire explode down the street.

"Damn! We just left from down there!" I said in frustration.

"There wasn't anybody outside," my partner added.

Scrambling back to the car, we slowly headed down the street with our lights off. Despite the street still being empty, I could feel the presence of danger in the air. Suddenly, a gang member armed with a gun stepped out of the shadows. As the gang member and I made eye contact, I could see by the wideness of his eyes he was startled by our presence. It didn't take long for him to regain his composer and run between some houses. My partner immediately slammed on the brakes. Like always, I was off and running before the car could come to a complete stop. This time officers responding to our back-up request arrived within seconds. I could hear the sound of tires screeching around the block and coming to a skid as a perimeter was formed around the area. By the time I climbed over the first fence, the suspect had disappeared in the shadows of a backyard. I was certain

145

he was hiding somewhere in one of two backyards because there were officers standing-by on the next street just seconds after our back-up request.

At first I thought we were just chasing another gang member with a gun which I had routinely done but then I heard the dispatcher broadcast a call of a homicide which just occurred down the street from where I first saw the armed gang member. There was no doubt in my mind the guy I was chasing was the murderer. Minutes later another radio call came out about a prowler in the rear yard of a house located two houses from our location. I was certain my 187 suspect was hiding in that yard.

I wanted to immediately apprehend the suspect before he could climb through someone's window and create a hostage situation. I randomly selected six officers and formed a search team. Coincidentally, all six of the officers involved on the search team were Black men. Officer Washington was the senior officer of the team. He had just recently passed the sergeants exam and was placed on the waiting list as one of the top ten candidates to become a sergeant. It was only a matter of time before he would become a sergeant. All he had to do was keep his nose clean.

Before entering the backyard where the suspect was hiding, I reminded everyone the suspect had already killed one person.

"Don't expect him to give up easily!" I added.

Officer Washington, who was armed with a shotgun, took the point position on the search team. Using hand signals for communication, the search team slowly crept into the dark yard. Trees and shrubs shielded the moonlight and officers

146

could barely see past their noses in the darkness. Suddenly, the bushes shook violently as a cat scrambled over the fence.

Boom! My ears rattled and my eyes burned from gunpowder thrust into the air by Officer Washington's shotgun. A streak of bright muzzle flash shot out of the barrel of his shotgun as the kickback caused him to fall backwards on the ground. Quickly helping him up off the ground, I ordered the search team to pull back out of the yard and retreat to a safe area.

Once we were in a safe area, I asked Washington, "What in the world were you shooting at?"

Washington just stood there in shock. His eyes and mouth were wide open. "I don't know. The gun just went off. I don't know what happened" he explained.

"Guns just don't go off by themselves dummy!" another officer said.

"You have to pull the trigger idiot!" one more added.

"I'm sorry fellas. I can't explain it. Damn! I'm never going to become a sergeant now," he said disappointedly with his head down.

"Nope, you sho won't. They look for any excuse to keep us from promoting," one officer added.

"That's true," I said. "I'll tell you what, if you guys don't say anything then I won't either."

"I'm down," another said. "There isn't anyway they can prove an officer fired the shot because people shoot in the air around here all night. Nobody even gets out of bed and looks out the window or calls the police anymore."

"Thanks fellas. I appreciate this," Washington said.

147

"When you become a sergeant, you better not become an jerk like all the rest," I said.

All six officers including myself agreed not to tell anyone about the accidental discharge of the shotgun. Eventually, the K-9 unit conducted a search of the area and located the suspect two houses away from where the accidental discharge occurred. Six hours later Officer Washington walked into the station to go home and passed by the watch commanders' office. The watch commander, unaware of Washington's accidental discharge, asked him, "I heard that there was some excitement out there tonight. What happened at that shooting back-up?"

As tears began to roll down his cheek, Washington confessed, "I'm sorry sir! I didn't mean to pull the trigger. It was an accident. The other five officers are not responsible. Don't punish them!"

The watch commander became upset. "What! You had an accidental discharge of a shotgun and didn't tell anyone? And other officers knew about it but didn't tell either?" he asked.

Everyone from the captain on down to the janitor was pissed off at Officer Washington. He received a fifteen-day suspension without pay and all the other officers involved received two-day suspensions for not rolling over on him. The other officers were so mad at Washington they all wanted to get together and beat him down. I declined to take the issue any further because I figured like before, someone would tell.

With this heavy burden on my mind, I was then required to go back out on the street to "protect and serve" the community. I was furious by the whole incident. The last thing

I wanted to do was work. Fighting crime was the furthest thing from my mind. I wasn't in the mood for the every day madness that took place. In my current state I knew it was only a matter of time before someone got hurt.

The following night, I was working with another Black officer while my regular partner was off duty. After roll call, as everyone was putting their equipment bags into the Black and White patrol cars, I was approached by two angry officers who were also involved in the prior night's incident.

"Hey, let's meet up somewhere for coffee as soon as we gas up," one said.

"That's cool with me. How about you partner?"

Pointing to several White officers who were congregating and spitting tobacco by the gas pumps, my partner replied, "That's cool with me too but let's not go where they always go. I don't feel like being around them racist cops!"

My partner was referring to a 7-Eleven store on Figueroa St. and Adams Blvd. It was almost a Southwest tradition for patrol officers to drive to the Seven Eleven and get a free cup of coffee immediately out of roll call. The Seven Eleven was often referred to as the "second roll call" because sometimes the whole watch would be there at once.

"All right then, let's meet up at the AM/PM mini-market on Crenshaw in twenty minutes."

Twenty minutes later my partner and I pulled into the parking lot of the mini-market and were greeted by two other patrol units who were waiting for our arrival. It was weird seeing four Black officers standing beside patrol cars drinking coffee. My partner and I were going to make it six.

149

"What's up house negro?" is how we were greeted.

"Negro? I ain't' heard that in a long time. What's up hommie?"

"Ain't no thang but a chicken wang!"

"Damn! There are too many Black officers here for me," one joked. "We better get us a White boy over here quick or somebody's gonna call the police and say, "I think some gang members stole some LAPD uniforms and are robbing the market."

"About last night, how come White boys can get away with stuff like that everyday and we do it once and get caught?" a participant asked me.

"I don't know. My mother always told me that we are our own worst enemies. I guess it's the same reason why Black citizens treat us worse than they do White officers."

"Slave mentality baby, slave mentality!"

Changing the subject, one officer asked another, "So who are you working with next month?"

"Some female named Parker. I don't know who she is but
she's   that nice looking Black babe that works day watch. I think she's a dyke!"

"How do you know?"

"Because I always see her giggling and rubbing up on Sherry. And we all know she's a dyke!"

"What else is new? Half the chicks on the department are lesbians."

"Do you know who gets all the women? Sergeant Kimberly Jackson. That girl be turning out all the women in the division. A brother don't stand a chance. I've seen her mack

150

down women and get the digits. Her rap is harder than any dude's that I've ever seen."

"I just wanna watch! She's healthy!"

While the officers were immersed in their deep and stimulating conversation, I noticed another patrol car approaching. Inside the car were two White police officers.

Leaning out the window, one of the passing officers yelled out, "How come we weren't invited? Is this one of those Black things you guys are always talking about? What are you guys doing, slinging bean pies?"

Holding up the middle finger, two officers yelled back, "Take this," as the patrol car passed by.

"I hate those redneck crackers!"

"They control the whole department! A brother can't get a promotion unless he goes out drinking with um!"

The following night, I still felt tired and dejected. When my partner came back to work, we started taking sabbaticals by parking in front of a Mexican bar on 41st St. and Figueroa. While parked, I gawked at tipsy women leaving the bar dressed in tight imitation leather dresses. My partner cursed the Department for everything he could think of.

"Maybe I should have knocked him on his butt!" I said out loud. "Naw. It was my fault too. I hate this job. I hate the officers, the citizens, the administration, the City Council, my fifth grade teacher,..."

BOOM! BOOM! BOOM! BOOM! BOOM! BOOM! Six thunderous gunshots rang out a few feet behind us while I was in the middle of venting my anger. Ducking down, I looked in the rear view mirror and saw a gangbanger standing in the street holding a smoking revolver in his hand. The gangbanger

151

then made a dash down the street, clawing his way through the departing club crowd.

When I was a teenager, my driving instructor told my class they should never drive a car when they were upset because anger would cloud their judgment. The same rule applied to police work. At that moment my judgment was clouded by anger.

I'm not chasing a suspect; I'm chasing my old training officer who told the captain I was a racist, I thought. No, this is my third grade teacher who told my father I was talking in class. This is for Cheezy.

Thinking my partner was going to follow me, the chase was on. After clearing the crowd, the gangbanger tossed his empty gun in some bushes and continued to run across Figueroa St. and through some apartment buildings. I relentlessly chased the assailant at top speed for three blocks and over four, eight-foot fences before he tired and slowed down in a dark alley crossing 43rd St. Sheer determination was on my mind. I was determined to make the gunman pay for every bad thing that had ever happened to me. My mind was running wild with crazy thoughts as I gained ground.

When I came within a few inches of the suspect, I clinched my flashlight and summoned up all of my fading strength. Raising my flashlight back, I took a wide swooping swing at the gunman's head. Fortunately, for us both, the gunman stumbled, lost his balance and fell to the ground before my flashlight could clip his cranium. Now straddling him and gritting my teeth, I again raised my flashlight and carefully aimed at his head. My intentions were to crack his head open. Just as I was about to crown him like a king, I heard a

152

police siren and tires screeching. Then, I saw a pair of bright head lights round the corner and rapidly come right at me.

Standing straight up and waving my hands, I screamed, "Stop!"

Rubber and brakes screamed so loudly my ears went deaf. I leaped into the air seconds before impact. I then landed on the top of the patrol car hood and rolled off onto the pavement. When I opened my eyes, I was surprised to see I was still in one piece. The suspect was once again running down the alley but he was so exhausted that the responding officers apprehended him in seconds.

I thanked God I failed in all my attempts to hit the gangbanger. If I had hit him, I probably would have seriously injured him. I realized my anger and violent behavior toward the suspect were not a result of the gunman's actions. My behavior was a result of all the compounded frustrations I had experienced since coming on the job. South Central LA was smothering me. Working and living in the same area was beginning to take its toll on me.

Even though the grace of God had saved me from committing one horrible act, my thoughts and intentions were still bad. The old adage, "What goes around, comes around" would soon hold true for me. All sorts of bad things started happening to me for no apparent reason. My only explanation was that somebody was trying to tell me something. I wasn't right inside.

THEM OR US

"Long ago I had come to realize that when an incident involved a black person, race is often interjected and can become a significant factor when really it shouldn't be."

Former LAPD chief Daryl Gates upon learning about the Rodney King beating. ("My life in the LAPD, Chief Daryl F. Gates" July 1992)

"Where is everybody?" my partner asked.

"I don't know. This is unusual. There are usually a lot more people on the street than this!"

As we drove slowly around the dark narcotic infested neighborhood of 43rd St. and Hoover St., we noticed only one young man standing on the corner. At midnight this particular corner was usually saturated with dirty and funky smelling, transient cocaine addicts. Shopping carts containing all of their worldly possessions would inconveniently block the sidewalks and the curb lane. This night the corner was virtually empty except for one young man in his early twenties. The young man was neatly dressed in a designer letterman jacket, blue jeans and Timberland boots. Staring at the patrol car as it passed, he suspiciously placed both hands underneath his jacket.

"You see that guy partner?"

Unenthusiastically, I replied, "Yeah, I see him."

"What do you think he's hiding?"

"Oh, a gun or some dope."

"You wanna stop him?"

"Nope!"

When we drove near the man, he turned and darted between some houses. "Oh well, he's gone now!"

As if nothing unusual had happened, we continued to slowly drive down the street looking for something more exciting and worthwhile. Ten minutes later we made a second pass by the corner of 43rd St. and Hoover St. To our surprise the same guy was still standing on the corner. This time he held up his middle finger and yelled something rude toward us. He then trotted slowly back between the houses.

"What's his problem?" my partner asked.

"I don't know. Maybe he's got a lot on his mind.," I reasoned.

"You wanna talk to him?"

"Naw. Not now. If he's still here later on tonight then we can stop *um*."

After patrolling the area for another thirty minutes, we once again rounded the corner and spotted the same gentleman with his hands wedged in his jacket pockets. With a frown on his face he gave us an angry look. This time he didn't so much as flinch as we neared.

"Okay partner, let's do this!" I said.

As soon as we exited the patrol car, the man casually walked back between the houses.

"What?" he asked.

My partner quickly drew his gun and trotted after him. "Don't move!"

"Who me?"

"Who? There's nobody around but you idiot!"

"Oh!" he replied.

Obeying the command, the guy froze and then complied with the rest of the officer's orders. While my partner searched him, I assumed the role of the covering officer. For precautionary reasons I surveyed every inch of the dark area, high and low for any signs of trouble. As we conducted our task between the two-story homes, out of the corner of my eye, I noticed an elderly woman in a rocking chair carefully watching our every move from a small second-story window.

"He's clean! What do you want to do with him?" my partner asked.

"Nothing. We can kick *um* loose. I'm hungry anyway." Turning back to the man who was standing facing the wall with his hands interlaced behind his back and legs spread apart, my partner forcefully said, "Go home! Don't let me see you hanging out on that corner anymore tonight!"

"Okay. No problem officer. I'm going straight home!"

We left the man between the houses and jumped back into the patrol car. We then headed toward the local convenience store for a complementary soda.

"I wonder why he was acting so weird?"

"I don't know. Maybe he was on drugs or just crazy."

"Who knows and who cares!"

Fifteen minutes later, we received a message over the car computer ordering us to return to the station and see the watch commander in his office as soon as possible. As ordered we immediately turned around and headed back to the station.

"What do you think the sergeant wants?"

"I don't know. We haven't handled any calls so it can't be related to a call."

156

When we got back to the station, the look on the sergeant's face was intense and serious. For whatever reason we were summoned back, we assumed it wasn't for a happy occasion.

"What's up Serg?"

Without smiling he answered, "I want you to go out into the lobby and tell me if you've seen that guy sitting on the bench before."

From behind the desk counter I looked into the front lobby of the police station and saw the young man from 43rd St. sitting on the lobby bench. The man was holding a towel up to his face. The young man's appearance had taken a dramatic change since we had left him on 43rd St. and Hoover St. Both eyes were swollen. His bloodied nose was turned a quarter to the left and blood steadily flowed from lacerations on his lips.

"Hey! We just got through talking to that guy," I said.

"Boy! What happened to him? Did someone beat him up after we left him?"

"Don't tell me he wants us to take the report? Forget it! He's a jerk!" I added.

The sergeant looked us square in the eye and answered, "He says that you guys dragged him between two houses and beat the crap out of him!"

My heart sunk down to the pit of my stomach as I looked at my partner for an explanation. It was obvious we had been setup. The problem was that I knew the captain wouldn't believe my story after the suspension I took the previous month for not reporting an officer's accidental discharge of a shotgun.

157

"So what happened out there?" the sergeant asked me.

"Um, nothing sir. We just saw this guy on the corner."

"And?"

"And he gave us the finger."

"And?"

"And then he ran between some houses."

"And?"

"And, I don't want to say anything else without a police representative or an attorney," I concluded.

"That's a wise decision!"

As the sergeant walked away shaking his head, I remembered the old lady in the window. She had to have seen the whole thing take place. The problem was I seriously doubted she would speak on our behalf, especially after all the bad publicity LAPD had received over the recent years. She could either speak out on our behalf or not say anything for the fear of retaliation, which wouldn't do us any good, or she could backup the victim's claim. Either way, I had no choice but to use her as a reference.

Damn! I bet that's why she was sitting in the window. She's probably in on it!

"Hey Serg! There was an elderly lady sitting in the window above where we stopped this guy. She saw the whole thing."

My partner who was unaware of her presence asked, "What lady? I didn't see a lady."

My partner's doubt raised more skepticism in the sergeant's mind. "What is she going to tell me?"

"I don't know."

158

"If she doesn't come out and say that you guys didn't beat him then you guys are in serious trouble. You might be looking at an indictment. The way it looks right now, it's not good."

I had done so many other violent acts and now I was about to get unjustly burned for something I didn't do. Three weeks later the sergeant approached me with the findings of his investigation.

"I spoke to the woman in the window that night. She said that she saw you guys stop that guy and talk to him. She said that you guys didn't do anything wrong, and after you left some of his friends beat him up. In fact, she was happy to see you. She asked me to tell you guys to come by more often to run off the dope heads."

I breathed a sigh of relief at the good news. I really didn't know what to think because I was still angry about the allegation I brutalized a citizen.

Should I damn all the citizens for what happened or should I give them special praise because of what the old lady did for me? I wondered.

For some reason the sergeant seemed a little disappointed by the fact I was out of trouble. Even though I was currently out of the doghouse, it wouldn't be long until I was there again.

Soon afterwards I was temporarily paired up with a young brother from the east coast. His Philadelphia accent was strong and easily recognizable. As we casually cruised around the division, my partner spotted a simple vehicular violation.

159

"That car in front of us has expired tags. Let's pull it over so I can write this guy a ticket."

"I don't know partner, traffic stops are bad luck for me. Every time I write a ticket I get a personnel complaint."

"I can't let this one go partner. His registration is overdue by three years. If I have to pay for mine, he's gotta pay for his. Don't worry. It won't take long," he promised.

Reaching down to the console, I flipped a switch that caused the yellow lights on top of the patrol car to continually flash on and off while the siren sharply chirped with loud volume.

Picking up the microphone, I broadcasted, "Three Adam fifteen, show us on a traffic stop on Crenshaw Blvd. and Vernon Ave. on a 1977 GMC Pacer!"

Once the car pulled over, my partner had the driver step out and walk onto the sidewalk where I awaited. The driver was a tall, angry, twenty-eight year old Black man. Unimpressively, he was dressed in a light blue leisure suit and wearing scuffed up black shoes. A slight odor of alcohol radiated from his breath as he grinned and yelled in my face.

"Well, well, I should have known it would be two so-called Black men pulling me over! Don't you *Oreos* have anything better to do than harass another Black man? Oh, I forgot. You're not Black."

"The reason we stopped you sir is because your registration is expired by three years."

"So what! Isn't there a robbery or something going on?"

I was determined not to respond to his verbal attacks because he wasn't saying anything I hadn't heard before. I just

160

wished my partner would hurry. Unfortunately for me, my partner chose to drag on the traffic stop by looking through the man's car. While he continued his investigation, I was forced to listen to the motorist's personal attacks.

"How much money do you make? I bet I make twice as much money as you do!"

Figuring casual conversation might relax his mouth, I asked, "So where you coming from tonight sir?"

"Your momma's house! The hooker told me to tell you hello when I was with her!"

To myself I thought, *Oh no. He didn't just talk about my mama. I know he didn't go there! Aw, shoot!*

Playing the dozens, bagging, capping or whatever you wanted to call it, was a forte of mine. Back in the day, my friends and I would talk about each other's mothers to the point where someone would start crying and then start swinging. But that was then, and now I was at work and had to maintain a professional demeanor.

"Your momma got some good loving, you know that officer?"

Gently touching the man's sleeve with my fingers, I asked, "This is a nice suit sir. Isn't this the same kind of suit the six-million dollar man wore in 1974?"

"Oh you think you're funny?" he said.

"I'm not trying to be funny. I loved to watch the *Bionic Man* in the seventies."

"You know what?" he asked.

"What?"

"I've probably got more money in my pocket than you make in a week.," he boasted

"So what do you do, Colonel Steve Austin?"

"Funny! I'm an attorney!" he responded.

"An attorney! An attorney and you can't even afford to pay the registration on a Pacer? What is it? About seventeen bucks? That's about what you paid for your shoes right?"

"I'll pay it when I'm damn ready!" the man snapped.

"So you're an attorney huh?

"You're damn right I am!" he shouted.

"Times must be hard. I guess O.J. laid you off, huh?"

The smirk on the man's face faded into a pitiful looking frown. His eyes began to blink faster and faster as he could no longer look me in the eye.

"I want to speak to a supervisor!" he demanded.

Oh shoot! I thought. *I think I took it too far.*

"Why do you want to speak to a supervisor?"

"I wanna make a complaint on you for being rude and unprofessional!"

As he requested, I had a supervisor come to the location of the traffic stop. The sergeant who arrived was a brand new sergeant with a week of sergeant's experience under his belt. When the sergeant arrived, he and the traffic violator stepped away from the scene. From a distance I could see the man adamantly moving his hands and making gestures while he spoke. When he concluded, the sergeant turned around and walked toward me. I knew I was wrong and was ready to face the music. I figured I'd get suspended for about two days. That didn't bother me because a suspension day was just another day off for me. No big deal.

"Well officer. His allegation is pretty serious."

"I know sir. I don't know what to say sir."

162

"I can't believe that he expects me to believe that you called him a racial slur."

"Huh?" I responded in shock.

"Yeah, he said you called him a Black, 'you know what,' and then you told him that he needed to go back to Africa."

"Are you sure he said that sir?" I questioned.

"Positive! Then he made his self look even more stupid by telling me you called him the 'Six-million dollar man.' Isn't that the same kind of suit the 'Bionic Man' wore?" the sergeant asked.

"I don't know Serg. That show was before my time. I don't think I've ever seen the show before."

"Don't worry about it. This guy is under the influence. I know that you wouldn't be stupid enough to talk about his shoes and his car. Nothing is going to happen to you."

Fortunately, I didn't get punished for the man's accusations. The thing that disturbed me the most was that the man falsely accused me of calling him a out of his name. The motorist probably figured he was adding fuel to the fire by claiming I called him a forbidden word. That just made things worse for him and all others who righteously made that complaint against the police.

Over the years, I had heard gang members say some White officers called them racist names. Although I had worked with these officers and assumed they would not have said what they were accused of saying, the accusations still caused me to internally question the White officers and look at them differently. There were so many false allegations reported against officers that no one believed the allegations

163

when they really happened. It is almost impossible to tell what a police officer's prejudices are by the way we treat citizens. When angered or stressed, a police officer may treat everyone badly.

The following night, my partner called the watch commander and advised him he was going to be about a half-hour late. Police officers hated working the front desk but that was my assignment until my partner could arrive from home.

The phones were ringing off the hook. The front lobby was hot and crowded with impatient people as Mondays were usually like that. People returned home from weekend vacations to find their homes, cars, and businesses burglarized or cars stolen. Some decided to wait until then to report their spouse had been beating on them all weekend.

A long line stretched through the lobby and out the front door. My attitude was not at its best because I hated working the desk. I considered myself a field soldier or as the Black officers joked, "a field negro" and at the front desk, I was far from being that. Taking reports and answering phones was not my idea of crime fighting.

About an hour into the watch, my head was buried in a report I was taking from a women whose checks were forged on her bank account. It was a desk officer's nightmare! It seemed that as soon as I walked up to the front desk, each of the three desk officers left and disappeared somewhere in the station and leaving me with the forgery report. From there a large number of people walked into the station with reports to make. I was pissed off and very impatient as I witnessed the line growing longer by the minute.

"Where in the hell is everybody else?" I questioned.

Out the corner of my eye, I saw a large hulking figure suddenly shield the light in the doorway. The man walked through the lobby door and continued to move past the waiting crowd in my direction. Before I could look up, I saw the shadow standing over me. The shadow belonged to a six foot six inch, 270-pound man casually dressed in a nylon sweat suit and high-top basketball shoes.

Rudely interrupting my conversation with the forgery victim, the man said, "Excuse me officer, I need to talk to you!"

Looking up at the man, I asked, "What is it sir? Do you have a quick question that I can answer for you?"

"No, not really. I want to talk to you about something. It might take awhile."

"Can't you see that I have a lobby full of people sir? You're going to have to wait in line like everyone else!"

"Oh, I'm sorry officer. I don't know what I was thinking about."

Patiently, he waited in line for ten minutes before he again charged back up to the front counter. "Officer, I really need to talk to you!"

"About what sir?"

"I have a little situation."

"Everybody in the lobby has a situation. Why's yours any more important than anyone else who's in line?"

"I'm not saying that it is officer. I just don't know what to do. I'm sorry. I'll get back in line and wait."

The impatient citizen took his place back in line. Turning my attention back toward the victim in front of me, I said, "Some people have a lot of nerve. He could see that I was in the middle of a report. How rude and inconsiderate!"

165

"I know what you mean officer." the immediate victim said. "These young people today have no manners. I wouldn't have even thought about walking in front of a line at a police station. Um um, no respect!"

Another ten minutes had passed before the big man got his chance to tell his story. By then I wasn't interested in what anyone had to say because I was tired of writing and I still had no help on the desk.

"It's about time officer. I was about to turn around and go back home."

"Why didn't you?"

"I know you're mad at me but I have to tell you something!"

"What is it sir?"

Smiling, he said, "I want to turn myself in."

Sarcastically I replied, "What do you want to turn yourself into, a woman?"

"That's funny!" he laughed. "It good to see an officer with a sense of humor."

The worse thing the man could have done was acknowledge my humor because now I was going to give him a double dose! "So, you want to turn yourself in for a warrant?"

"No not a warrant," he said with a smile.

"Sorry! Our jail is full right now. We're only taking felony arrests. If you have a traffic warrant you're going to have to go to traffic court and clear it up. The only way you're getting in our jail tonight is if you've killed somebody."

The man's laugh was loud and animated as he grabbed his stomach and rocked back at the waist. "You don't have to worry about me getting traffic warrants because I

166

always make sure I pay my tickets on time. That's a big deal to me. I don't wanna get arrested for warrants and spend a weekend in jail."

"So why are you here?"

"Actually, I want to turn myself in because I killed someone."

I couldn't believe he expected me to fall for that one, especially since I just told the man he could only go to jail for that reason. I immediately formed the opinion that I was dealing with a nut that wanted a place to sleep or some attention.

"Did this just happen sir?"

"No! Of course not. I wouldn't be this calm if it just happened officer. You're funny!"

"Okay, so when did you do it? Don't tell me you're one of America's most wanted?"

"You're crazy!" he laughed. "You've gotta stop joking so I can tell you what happened."

"Sorry, go ahead."

"I killed this woman two days ago."

I looked at the man and waited for a punch line that never arrived. "Saturday huh? Why are you coming in two days later?"

"Well, I was hitting her over the head with a baseball bat and she was running around the house screaming for help. Usually when we argue, the neighbors always call the police. After I realized that she was dead, I sat on the couch, watched the baseball game and waited for the police but you guys never came."

I still wasn't buying his story because the man was still smiling and giggling. I figured he was trying to top my humor. I had to admit, the big guy was brightening up my dreadful night.

"Well sir, you know LAPD, we're never around when you need us!"

"Ain't that the truth! So what are you going to do?"

"Where's the body? Is it still on the living room floor?"

"Oh no! I'm a tidy person. I cleaned up the blood, wrapped up the body in garbage bags and placed it in the hall closet."

Suddenly, my stomach started to knot up and a dry lump formed in my throat. What if he was telling the truth? Something wasn't right! The thought of me having a psychopathic killer standing in front of me caused my legs to tremble. I casually glanced around the lobby to see if any other officers were nearby. There were none. I didn't want to startle the suspect by broadcasting a back-up request for a murder suspect over the station P.A. system.

Trying my damnedest to remain a humorist, I said, "Okay sir, I'll tell you what, since I like you and you laughed at my jokes, let's go in the back and talk about it in the officer's break room."

"Sure officer!" he replied with glee.

"Oh! I forgot our station policy is that I have to handcuff and search you first."

"No problem."

While I was searching him, my trembling hands came across a set of house keys in his pocket. "Are these the keys to your house sir?"

168

"Yep, take um and go to my house and see for yourself."

"Okay, after we have a cup of coffee."

I then lead him into the glass holding cell where suspects are kept temporarily until they are booked or released.

"Hey! This is not a break room officer. This is a cell," he stated.

"What? You mean to tell me that all this time I've been drinking my coffee in a jail cell? No wonder everybody I sit next to always asks me if I have a smoke and why are they here."

The suspect laughed and shook his head as he entered the cell to with the door slamming behind him. When my partner finally arrived at work. We got in our patrol car and drove to the suspect's home, which was just four blocks away from the police station.

"So what's this guy's story?" my partner asked.

"At first I thought he was crazy but then he started giving me this eerie feeling. I don't know if he's a loony or not. All I know is it's worth checking out."

"How come you always seem to attract problems?"

"Because I have horrible partners. If you would have come to work on time we wouldn't be handling this mess."

Within a few minutes we were at the murder suspect's residence. The man lived on a well-kept neighborhood street. Every home had neatly cut green grass and trimmed hedges. Bright, colorful paint highlighted each English style home. A couple of elderly senior citizens with canes and walkers slowly stepped down the sidewalk for exercise. It was hardly a place where a psychopathic killer would live.

The suspect's house was dark and looked uninhabited. Either no one was home or everyone was asleep or dead. As I walked up to the front door, I used my flashlight to illuminate my hand while I searched through the jumbled key ring. Flipping each one over, I checked to see if one resembled a door key.

"Maybe I should ring the door bell and see if anyone is home?"

"Somebody is here," my partner said.

"How do you know?"

"Cause I can smell them rotting inside a closet," he joked.

"I sure hope not. Maybe we should've grabbed a bite to eat first? Just in case."

Once the key was found, I put it in and fearfully turned the lock. The anticipation of finding a dead decaying body was enough to make me queasy.

"What if we walk inside and the corpse jumps out and tries to eat us?"

"I think you've been watching too much television."

Taking a small step through the door, I used my hand to feel around the wall for the light switch. *CLICK!* A light from a chandelier lit the front room. There wasn't anything special about the decor. It was just an average looking home. There wasn't anything in the room that would indicate a cold-blooded killer lived there.

Several feet from the door was a hall closet just like the suspect said there would be. My heart rate started to increase as we stepped closer to the hall closet. It didn't matter that I had seen a countless number of dead bodies. The suspense of finding a fresh corpse was always the same. It's like waking up on Christmas morning, walking into the living room, and wondering what Santa Clause brought you. I opened the closet door and held my breath in suspense.

"Well partner, there she is." I calmly said.

Just as the man had described, we found a large object about five feet, six inches long wrapped in a bunch of torn, green plastic garbage bags. The appearance of the figure was of a modern day ghetto mummy.

"Open her up partner!"

"Hell no!" I firmly stated. "I ain't opening up anything!"

"Somebody's gonna have to verify that it's a dead body. How do we know that it's not a mannequin or something?"

"I'll just take that guy's word for it. He hasn't lied to me so far."

My partner eagerly removed a sharp steel-folding knife from his back pocket and flipped it open. Kneeling down on one knee, he carefully made a small rectangular incision into the plastic. The decaying body conclusively told us the man sitting in the station holding cell was a murderer.

Our night was ruined and shot! It would take two hours for the homicide detectives to arrive and another six hours for the county coroner to arrive.

"I told you we should've gotten something to eat!"

"I wonder what he's got to eat in the frig?"

"Oh, probably an arm, leg, or human head."

171

The real joke was on me. What if my negative attitude had caused the suspect to leave the station in disgust or anger? It was a weird feeling knowing I came very close to ignoring a dangerous suspect's cry for help.

My partner and I nonchalantly exited the house to preserve the crime scene from further contamination of evidence. My partner walked back to the patrol car to notify the watch commander of our findings. Several minutes later, my partner returned to the house with a large roll of yellow crime scene tape. The officer tied one end to a pillar and stretched the roll across the porch where he tied the other end to a fence. Neighbors gradually started filing out of their homes and positioned themselves on the sidewalk in front of the house.

"I think we better throw some tape up across the lawn before folks invite themselves in."

"I think you're right. They're lining up like King Tut is in there."

My partner quickly picked up the crime scene tape and used trees, poles and bushes to box off the house. "Okay, I need everyone to remain behind the tape please." My partner said those words as a formality. People in South Central LA were accustomed to seeing crime scene tape and automatically stayed behind it unlike the naive people I had experienced in the West Los Angeles area.

Once while working in West LA, I was standing away from a dead body with yellow crime scene tape around it. A White person tapped me on the shoulder and politely said, "Excuse me officer but you left your tape around that red sheet. Do you want me to get it for you?"

"No thanks, I'll get it later," I smartly replied.

172

Homicide scenes are usually the worse place an officer could be. They are boring. Once the crime scene is sealed off, there is nothing else to do but wait. While waiting for the homicide detective's arrival, I daydreamed about my first homicide scene. I was nervous, nauseous, and frightened. I didn't know what in the hell was going on. Interestingly, detective Mark Fuhrman, who discovered the famous bloody glove at O.J.'s house, was one of the investigating detectives on the case. For two hours, I was forced to stand over a woman who had been beaten to death.

Another incident that popped in my mind was of the night Marlon Brando's son Christian Brando murdered his sister's boyfriend inside their mansion. After learning there was a homicide at Marlon Brando's estate, I asked my training officer if he wanted to go look at the body and check out the news reporters out front. I thought the atmosphere would be exciting.

"Hell no!" My partner answered. "Trust me, you don't want to get involved in that fiasco. The media will find some way to blame LAPD for the death." He then told me to make every effort to avoid responding to calls involving celebrities.

"They're nothing but trouble!" he told me.
At the time I didn't understand what my partner meant but I later learned from the O.J trial.

About an hour and a half into the crime scene, a young man approached the outskirts of the tape. We sensed something unusual about his curiosity. Finally, the young man approached us as we lounged back in the patrol car eating sunflower seeds.

"Excuse me officers, can I ask you something?"

173

"Sure sir, go ahead."

"I live next door. Does that yellow tape mean someone's dead inside?

"Yes sir it does."

"Can you tell me who it is?" the man asked.

"We don't know who the person is," I responded.

"Is it a woman?"

I looked at my partner before answering, "Why, something wrong?"

"Yeah, Friday my girlfriend called me and told me she was on her way over to my house. I left and went to the store to buy some food in case she got hungry. She never showed up and I can't get in touch with her. Nobody's seen her."

"Did you try calling her family?"

"She don't have any out here."

"Well, we don't know who the victim is but I'm sure it's not your girlfriend," I assured him.

The man sadly walked back into his house. I couldn't help but wonder if the woman inside wasn't the missing woman. It was too much of a coincidence. The whole day had been weird so why shouldn't it continue that way.

"So what do you think partner?"

"I think she probably found someone else on the way over to his house. She's probably getting laid as we speak."

"It could be some kind of love triangle or something."

"I doubt it!"

Four hours later, my partner and I were released from the crime scene to go home. We lugged our equipment bags in the station and dropped them against the wall closest to the parking lot door. As I walked to the kit room to turn in my

174

shotgun, I still wondered about the missing woman. I checked in my shotgun and then detoured to the holding cell where the murder suspect was still being held.

"Hey officer, did you find her?" he yelled through the thick glass.

"What's your girlfriend's name?" I shouted back.

"I don't know."

"Wait a minute. How can she be your girlfriend and you not know her name?" I asked. "Is she or is she not your girlfriend?"

"I guess she's my girlfriend. If she wasn't my girlfriend, why was she in my house?"

The new information was given to the homicide detectives. A few weeks later, I went to court to testify on the murderer. I was surprised to learn the victim was indeed the neighbor's girlfriend. The murderer saw her sitting on the porch and dragged her into his house where he strangled her to death. My testimony was occasionally broken up by the wailing cry of the victim's boyfriend. I felt funny because I had assured the man his girlfriend was not the victim. Suddenly that day wasn't very funny.

After testifying, I stepped off the witness stand and exited the courtroom. The victim's boyfriend matched me step for step. With tears still streaming from his eyes, he got my attention.

"Excuse me officer, can I talk to you for a second?"

"How can I help you?" I answered.

In a state of confusion, the man rambled, "What happened? Nobody will tell me anything! Why did he do it? Was she raped? I need someone to tell me something!"

175

"I'm sorry sir but I don't know any more than what I testified to. I'm sorry."

"Can you find out for me?"

"No I can't. Sorry."

I continued to walk down the hall. I lied. I could have found out for him but I had no desire to. The case was already too disturbing. I had told the story over and over to my friends and coworkers. Everyone thought it was funny. The new ending changed things dramatically.

UNFORTUNATELY, LAPD WAS NOT A SMOOTH RUNNING MACHINE LIKE TELEVISION SHOWS OFTEN PORTRAYED. Officers rarely got a chance to work together for a long period of time. Because of a large hiring boom, brand new officers right out of the academy were forced to work with officers who had little experience themselves.

One night, I was working with a guy who had only been out of the police academy six months. Many veteran officers took their time getting to calls and looked the other way when they worked with new officers. They didn't want to get into a life-threatening situation and find out their partner was unable to contribute. I figured I shouldn't be too concerned with my own safety because things had died down considerably over the last couple of months. The crime rate had dropped significantly.

Throughout the night, my partner and I talked about tactics and hypothetical situations. Like most new officers who weren't afraid, my partner was eager to jump into something. Having been there and done that, I knew exactly how he felt. In the beginning, it was all fun and games. Now I

176

was becoming hesitant. Putting myself into dangerous life threatening situations was beginning to fray my nerves. No matter how tough and heartless I was at work, like Freddy Krueger in "Nightmare on Elm Street," the demands would always win out in my nightmares.

Despite all of my doubts and concerns, a part of me still wanted to give the young buck a taste of excitement. My partner reminded me of myself when I first transferred over to Southwest Division.

Around 2:30 a.m., another unit was assigned a robbery in progress call at the Popeye's Chicken stand on the corner of Jefferson Blvd. and La Brea Ave.

"Hey partner, we're pretty close to that call. Let's go!" I said.

Ten minutes later we were pulling into an alley behind the establishment. Just as we pulled up, a man exited the front door of the chicken stand carrying a stuffed bag and a handgun. Without further ado, he immediately emptied his hands and took off running southbound across Jefferson Blvd. toward another alley.

"This is it baby! This is what you've been waiting for!" I yelled.

While my rookie partner froze and tried to figure out what to do next, I was off and running into the wind. The distance between the suspect and I was about fifty feet. From behind I could see he was medium height and lean. He was also appropriately dressed in a blue sweatshirt, tight football shorts that stopped just above his knee and fresh Nike Cross Trainer tennis shoes.

177

The suspect and I entered the alley. From a distance I could see that a nine-foot, wrought iron gate with spear shaped spikes on top of each bar, closed off the end of the alley. Judging by the suspect's appearance and desire to escape, I figured he could easily leap up to the top of the gate and flip over to the other side without getting seriously injured. There was no way in hell I was going to even try to go over the gate. I knew of an officer who had to have a testicle removed because he injured himself on a gate like the one I was fast approaching.

My only chance of nabbing the suspect was to catch him before he made it to the gate. Suddenly, the gate took on a new meaning. It wasn't just a gate, it was the gateway to freedom and the light at the end of the tunnel. I could tell the suspect already had this figured out because he was grunting loudly and groaning with effort. No matter how hard I tried to accelerate, my gear wouldn't allow my legs to shift into over-drive. All I could do was maintain the starting distance.

The suspect's effort was rewarded by him reaching the gate first. In a single leap he reached the top of the gate and grabbed a hold of a spike with each hand. Swinging his lower body upward, he managed to place his right foot on top of a spike without cutting himself. Then he quickly started pulling himself up.

I was in a win or lose situation. It was as if I was in the NBA Slam Dunk contest and needed a perfect score on a dunk to win. As I approached the gate in a last chance effort, I took two extra long steps and took off in flight like Michael Jordan dunking from the free throw line.

178

Arms swinging wildly, feet and legs walking through the air, I landed on the robber's back. My weight caused us both to fall off the gate and down to the ground. Unfortunately, I landed on the bottom of the stack. If I'd been at home, I would have laid on the ground and cried for at least ten minutes. Right now I had a robber on top of me so I couldn't.

Before I knew it, I was struck in the face by the robber's fist and then cracked in the jaw by an elbow. Bouncing to his feet, the robber gave me a swift kick in the ribs. Grabbing on to his leg, I pulled myself up and returned a punch or two. Removing my flashlight from my back pocket, I delivered an uppercut to the suspect's groin, not once but twice. Nothing happened as the fight was still on.

In a short time, we were both arm weary and tired. All we could do was clinch and hold onto each other like two obese heavyweight boxers. In the distance I could hear the unmistakable sound of my partner's keys jiggling as he ran down the alley. When I looked up, I saw my partner in mid air. His arms and legs were spread apart as he was about to do a belly flop on my head. Like a house made out of a deck of cards, we all tumbled to the ground upon the officer's impact. My partner then held on to the still struggling robber and handcuffed him.

Out of breath, I asked, "Is that what they teach you guys now in the academy?"

"No! I learned that by watching professional wrestling on TV."

After that arrest I didn't want to deal with any more probationers. I should have received a commendation for my

179

valiant effort but instead; I was rewarded with a lengthy internal affairs investigation for excessive force.

BORDER LINE

"We've got females and dumb Blacks and all your Mexicans that can't even write the name of the car they drive."

Former LAPD Detective Mark Fuhrman.. (From transcripts used by the O.J Simpson defense lawyers)

During the next deployment period, I watched my new partner stand on his tiptoes, take a deep breath, suck in his stomach and then strap on his gun. My new partner's uniform didn't fit him much better than any other twelve-year veteran. Officer Gonzales was a large, thirty-three year old, Mexican man with twelve years of service on the job.

Like myself, my partner was also on the captain's bad list. He had two prior drunk driving convictions and was currently driving on a restricted driving license, meaning he was only allowed to drive to and from work and during the course of employment.

My partner and I didn't get along too well. In my opinion he appeared to put more energy into talking victims out of making reports than trying to help them find the culprits. Eventually, I felt the need to express my concerns to him.

"Why do you always try to talk people out of making reports when they only take but a minute to do *um*?"

"Why are you Black officers always so angry?" He sarcastically responded.

"Why are Mexican officers always so complacent and so happy to conform with the White man? You are a minority just like me. If there weren't any Mexicans in LA you wouldn't have a job." I told him.

I was so quickly disturbed by my partner's remark because I had a similar conversation with another officer of Mexican decent several months prior. Then I had volunteered to work a cash overtime detail during the day watch. I was teamed up with a Mexican-American officer. As usual our first order of business was to get something to eat at Mc Donald's. As we approached the drive-through speaker in the Black and White, we heard an employee with a heavy Spanish accent ask us if he could take our order.

"Let me have one cheese burger!" My partner said.

The employee verified his order. "That's one chez bull-ger, yes?"

"I said cheese burger. What in the heck is a chez bull-ger?" He rudely questioned the employee.

Slowly enunciating each syllable, the employee repeated, "C.H.E.Z B.U.L.L-G.E.R, chez bull-ger."

"Aw forget it!" My partner yelled into the speaker. "How in the world did you get a job and you can't even speak English wet-back?"

Angered by his comments, I said, "Give the guy a break. At least he is trying to speak correctly and he is working for a living."

I then asked him how he could condemn someone who speaks broken English when his ancestors were immigrants to this country and probably faced the same problems as the Mc Donald's employee?

"I don't care what they did or what they went through. I was born here. I'm not Mexican-American, Latino or

182

Hispanic. I'm American!" He then proudly said, "I don't even know how to speak Spanish."

I shook my head and replied, "You're still a wet-back in the police department's eyes."

"Why are all you Black guys always so angry?" He asked. "Are you going to order anything?"

"Hell no!" I yelled, "Saliva is not part of my diet. You know that he's gonna spit on your bull-ger, don't you? You'll find out exactly what a chez bull-ger is. It's cheese on boogers."

"Talking into the speaker, he said, "That's okay, cancel the order, we have a call."

While Officer Gonzales and I bickered, we suddenly observed a car loaded up with gang members run a red light and almost collide with crossing traffic. I immediately hung a U-turn and followed the car a few blocks before pulling the gang members over near the corner of Jefferson Blvd. and Western Ave. Without a backup we then routinely ordered the four occupants out of the car and handcuffed each one of them. A thorough search of the car and the youthful gang members only uncovered a small amount of marijuana. Since the threat of danger was now determined to be minimal, my partner and I started a conversation with the gang members. The talk revealed the boys were members of the Rollin 30s crips.

The traffic stop location was sort of in the neutral zone of the Rollin 30s crips and their archenemies, the Rollin 20s bloods' neighborhood. As my partner began writing, the driver a ticket for running the red light, I continued to jaw with the still handcuffed gang members. Without warning rapid gunfire

183

exploded in our direction from an apartment rooftop across the street. Several rounds sizzled just above my head and bounced off of a telephone poll directly behind my partner. My partner and I instinctively dove behind the patrol car for cover. The euphoric gang members quickly crawled on the ground to their car in order to avoid the bullets ricocheting off the pavement in front of them. The sniper rotated between firing at us and the gang members. Picking up the microphone, my partner yelled, "Officer needs help, Western Ave. and Jefferson Blvd. Shots fired! Shots fired!"

Thirty seconds after radioing for help, I could hear the roar of the air unit approaching. Even with the air unit's quick response, the sniper disappeared from the rooftop unseen. An extensive search of the area by the K-9 unit could not turn up a suspect. My partner and I, along with the gang members and several other officers, stood around and held the crime scene until detectives could arrive from home and do an investigation. By now, my partner and the gang members were nervous wrecks. They constantly passed gas and smoked cigarettes to the butts in four puffs. When they ran out of smokes, they sent a neighborhood transient to the corner liquor store to buy some more.

I wasn't nervous but I felt ever so helpless and frustrated. For me this was the second time I had been shot at without being able to squeeze off a round in my defense. I quickly went from being the hunter of gang members to the hunted. The time in which the event took place was mind-boggling. This time it happened so fast I didn't get a chance to see where the shots originated. I could only speculate about the location and for whom they were meant. My guess was

184

that some blood gang member saw us on our stop and then saw an opportunity to kill two birds with one stone. Why not kill a cop and a crip at the same time?

Later that early morning, the captain of the division arrived at the crime scene from home. The captain looked concerned as he approached a group of officers who were watching the detectives do their investigation.

"Are you guys okay?" The captain asked with great concern. "I got out of bed and rushed down here as soon as I heard the news. Who was involved?"

The officers pointed to Officers Gonzales and me. The captain's facial expression changed dramatically as if to say, "I got out of bed and rushed down here to the ghetto for you two bums?"

"Is there anything that I can do for you guys?" he asked unconvincingly.

You can kiss my butt! I thought to myself as I smiled. "No thank you sir." I really answered.

"Are you sure?"

"Yes sir, I'm fine."

The detective's investigation turned up zilch! Whoever shot at us was gone in the wind without leaving a clue as to whom he was or if he was gang affiliated.

I couldn't sleep a wink that morning when I got off work. I was so antsy that I continuously paced the floor of my house until it was time to go back to work that night. Dark circles framed my eyes the next night. When my partner sat down in the patrol car and stared straight ahead, I noticed that his face and ears were bright red. He was frantically chewing a wad of gum and chugging down a 32 oz. cup of

185

coffee. Underneath the smell of cinnamon gum and coffee, reeked the smell of alcohol. Without a doubt last night's incident caused him to fall off the wagon. I wondered what I should do.

In the academy officers were taught to immediately notify a supervisor in this situation but there was no way I could have rolled over on a partner with whom I had just been through a life-threatening situation. Besides, I knew this was my partner's third strike and he would most likely get fired. He had a wife who didn't work and a young son to support. My suspicions went without mention. I made it a point not to get out of the car and handle any calls or do any major police work. My partner and I didn't argue once the whole night. All we talked about was the shooting that occurred the night before.

"If I get shot at tonight I'm quitting," I said.

I thanked God we made it through the night without any problems. I decided that if I smelled any alcohol on my partner's breath the next night, I was going to ask the watch commander if I could work at the desk and put the burden of reporting Gonzales on someone else. The next night Officer Gonzales was arrested for drunk driving while on his way to work.

My quarrels with Mexican-American police officers didn't end there. About a month later a Hispanic sergeant was angrily questioning my partner about a report he wrote. My partner was Afro-American.

Speaking on my partner's behalf, I said, "Excuse me sir, but..."

186

Before I could finish my sentence, the sergeant interrupted me. Pointing his finger in my face, he said, "Keep your mouth shut and speak when you're spoken to!"

My eyes and mouth popped wide open. *Aw man! He's talking to me as if I was his boy!*

Pointing my finger back in the sergeant's face, I replied, "You're not my father and I'm not your boy so don't point your finger in my face, and when I'm speaking, you listen!"

Needles to say, the sergeant didn't like this. For several weeks he followed me to every radio call, hoping to catch me doing something wrong so he could document it. Every time I called into work sick a sergeant would drive to my house and check to see if I was actually ill. That was one of the disadvantages of living in the same division as I worked.

My house was only two minutes from the station and part of the daily patrol route. The sergeant would always start off by saying, "Since I was in the neighborhood I decided to see how you were doing."

One night I called in sick because I just couldn't bare any more abuse. Suddenly my doorbell rang. Looking out the peephole, I saw it was the evil sergeant. Thinking quickly, I ran into my bathroom and splashed hot water on my face and popped a cough drop in my mouth. Pretending to be deathly ill, I opened up the door. Squinting my eyes, I touched the sergeant's face with my wet hands and breathed mentholated breath into the sergeant's face.

In a faint voice I asked, "Serg, is that you?"

187

Holding his breath and turning his head, the sergeant abruptly pushed my hand away and stepped back. "Get some rest," he told me as he disappointedly walked away. I knew he was hoping to catch me working out or doing something so he could suspend me.

I couldn't recall ever hearing any officers say a sergeant drove to Orange County to see if they were all right. Finally, one day in roll call, that same sergeant told the watch he had some information regarding a suspect who was wanted for robbery. The sergeant described the suspect as being a male Black between five feet six and five feet eight inches tall, nothing else. The sergeant looked up and noticed no one was writing down the information. Directing his attention toward me, he asked, "Why aren't you writing this information down?"

"Sir, I didn't write the information down because it's a general description of almost everyone in the division," I replied.

Immediately after roll call the sergeant initiated a personnel complaint against me. In his opinion I had referred to all the suspects in the division as being Black men and he was offended by my so-called racist remarks.

I was so pissed off that I refused to read and initial his written statement. I also refused to respond to any of his questions without legal representation present. This caused him to become angrier. The sergeant's anger resulted in another complaint of insubordination which if found guilty was punishable by termination.

Patrol officers often twisted the truth around on arrest reports in order to get their suspects convicted. Sergeants

188

fabricated the truth on personnel complaints in an attempt to suspend or terminate patrol officers. Like a judge, the captain was more inclined to believe the accuser than the officer in question. The irony of it all was that I spent five years trying to escape being labeled as anti-White only to get punished for allegedly being racist toward my own people. What made things even more confusing was the complaint was initiated by a non-Black sergeant.

Several years prior, it was a racial remark that got me in trouble while on probation at West LA Division. Then I was accused of being racist toward Whites by a Black captain. Now I was accused of being racist toward Blacks by a pseudo Hispanic officer who only admitted being Hispanic on promotional exams.

What in the hell is going on? I asked myself.

189

WRONG PLACE

"You just don't even understand. This job is not rules. This is a feeling. Skip the rules: we'll make them up later."

Former LAPD Detective Mark Fuhrman. (Based on transcripts used by the O.J Simpson defense lawyers)

I was confused and mentally exhausted, so when I went home I immediately collapsed in front of the television set. The top story on the news was about a disgruntled employee who went on a rampage and killed several of his coworkers.

Not a bad idea. I know a couple of sergeants that I'd like to kill.

With that thought in mind, I drifted off to sleep. As usual, my dreams took over my subconscious mind. This time I didn't dream of the foot pursuit or the shots fired. Instead, I saw myself smiling while sitting at my kitchen table. I had a sheet of paper and a pencil in my hand. Interestingly, I was carefully compiling a list of the top ten people I wanted to kill. As I wrote down each name, their faces appeared in my mind.

My first grade teacher headed the list. Mrs. Martin was responsible for my first school related beating. My mother seized the moment and spanked my butt with her pink slipper. Second on the list, was my fifth grade teacher who caused me to get my first school related beating and punishment combo. The rest of the list consisted of a few sergeants and my former training officer from West LA Division. Finally, the evil sergeant from Southwest Division ended the list. He was last because I wanted to torture him before killing him.

My victim's screams awakened me. Sitting up in bed, I looked around the room and felt a little disappointed that I was only dreaming. I was distressed because I feared one day I may have a drink and turn my fantasy into a reality. What was even more frightening was that I could have probably talked a few officers into helping me carry out my plan. I knew of other officers who were potentially homicidal and mentally disturbed. Like me, each was a time bombs waiting to explode!

I was starting to hate my job. I could see why LAPD lost approximately one hundred officers a year to other law enforcement agencies. If LAPD's motto to the community was: "To protect and serve," then the officer's motto to each other should have been: "Every man and woman for himself." LAPD was a cold organization. If for some reason a supervisor disliked an officer, the supervisor would spread vicious rumors and lies around the department to other supervisors. Once a person was on the bad list, he was screwed for years.

I would look through the classified ads in the newspaper for a new job every Sunday. I wanted to leave the headache altogether. I didn't want another job in law enforcement but for some reason, no other job interested me. I felt similar to a man who was in a bad relationship with his woman but was afraid to leave because he was "whipped." I hated the relationship I had with my superiors but I was addicted to the five minutes of excitement that often came with the job. Where else could I wake up in a bad mood and then take it out on people?

191

When I returned to work the next day, I found a ten-day suspension and an unsatisfactory performance evaluation waiting for me. During the evaluation period, I had received three commendations for performing over and beyond the call of duty. I was probably the only person in LAPD history with five years of field experience to receive an unsatisfactory performance evaluation. The most sickening part of it was that my sergeant didn't have the guts to hand the bad news to me personally. Just before roll call a lieutenant approached me with the bad news.

"I'm sorry that you have to come to work and receive bad news. I heard that you've been having problems with a particular sergeant. In the event that you decide to hurt someone, I just want you to know that I think you are a good officer so aim the other way please," he told me.

The lieutenant smiled and dropped the papers in front of me before scurrying away. I was so furious after reading my evaluation that I stormed out of roll call and went straight to the patrol captain's office. When I arrived at the captain's office, I was disappointed to find his office door open. On the way there I fantasized about kicking it open.

The captain was in his first year as a patrol captain. His first day at Southwest Division, he came into roll call and fed officers a bunch of bull about how he was a patrol officer's captain, meaning he stood by his field officers.

"I need to talk to you!" I demanded in a hostile tone.

"I need to talk to you too," he replied.

I took a seat and prepared for battle. "I've been looking at your personnel complaint and your performance

192

evaluation. At the rate you are going, you're not going to be on this job long," he said.

"What are you talking about?" I yelled. "Anybody with any time on the job knows this is bull. If my performance is unsatisfactory then 99.9% of the officers in this division are also unsatisfactory. How can someone say that my comment was improper when White officers mimic and make minority jokes all the time?"

Scratching his head and looking puzzled, the captain asked, "They do? When did they start doing this?"

"Oh, sometime in the 1800's," I smartly replied. "You're full of it captain!"

After several minutes of arguing back and forth, the captain decided to substantiate my personnel complaint. My feelings were hurt. I felt unappreciated. I wanted someone to show me a little appreciation for risking my life every night to help others. Instead, the captain thanked me with a ten-day suspension for my efforts. The citizens of the division thanked me by calling me "Uncle Tom", "sell out and a "bald headed punk!" My spirit had finally been broken. I felt like lowering my head and saying, "My name is Toby!"

My next order of recourse was to write an appeal to police Chief Willie Williams. Up until now I hadn't given the new chief much thought. The chief was also in his first year. That worried me because I hadn't had much luck with newly promoted supervisors.

Many officers believed the new chief was not qualified for the job and that he was only appointed to the position as a puppet for the City Council. The rumor circulating among the Black officers was that as a police commissioner in

193

Philadelphia, he made examples out of the Black police officers. He was known for giving them the maximum penalties for misconduct while letting White officers off easy. The rumor sounded familiar. I was made an example while on probation at West LA Division. I figured my goose was cooked! I appealed only as a formality.

Several months later I was approached by the watch commander who was holding a sheet of paper in his hand. I naturally assumed it was another personnel complaint.

"The chief dismissed your suspension. It's all over," he told me.

I couldn't believe my ears. Basically, the chief viewed the allegations as I did, "A complete waste of time!" It was a rare deed for a chief of police to rule against a captain and a sergeant regarding a personnel complaint. Delighted is how I felt as I eagerly initialed the order. Later that night I joyfully relayed the news to one of my White coworkers.

"Oh, so you mean that the chief squashed the complaint because you're both Black, right?" he said.

Raising my fist in the air, I proudly responded, "That's right! Willie is my hommie and it's a Black thang; you wouldn't understand."

"I know that if that complaint was made against me he would have hammered me," the White officer replied.

"Maybe, but there's a good chance that the complaint wouldn't have been made. The sergeant was offended because I made the remark. He probably would have thought it was funny if you had said it."

"You're probably right. Forget it!"

194

MAKING A POINT

"See, if you did the things that they teach you in the academy, you'd never get a thing done."

Former LAPD Detective Mark Fuhrman. *(Based on transcripts used by the O.J Simpson defense lawyers)*

After working a year and a half on the mid PM. watch, I was moved to PM watch which was from 3:00 p.m. to 11:00 PM. Although this was the busiest watch, in contrast, it consisted of some of the laziest officers in the division.

My new partner was a fifteen-year veteran with ten of those years coming from Southwest Division. He was a mild-mannered, well-groomed, middle-aged Black man with a medium John Shaft afro and side burns. He was one of those brothers who refused to give up the seventies look. The only thing missing was a black leather coat, which he probably wore on the weekends. Every time I saw him, I couldn't help but think of the theme song from the movie *Shaft*.

My first impression of him was, "Anyone in his forties who still sported an afro and side burns must have an identity problem." The seventies were over!

My new partner did everything slowly. He talked, walked, filled out the daily log slowly, and typed on the computer slowly. At first, I thought he was lazy. Politely speaking with a southern accent, my partner asked me to drive so he could sit back and enjoy the sites.

"What sites?" I asked. "This is South Central LA. What in the hell are you going to look at transients?"

195

"There's a lot to see if you just take the time to look," he replied.

"I've been living here for years and I haven't seen a thing."

"That's because all you young guys ever look for is the bad stuff. I'm from Alabama. Where I'm from we take our time and look at everything."

The first thing I did was head straight to *The Jungle* to take care of some unfinished business. Since almost becoming a statistical victim of a drive-by shooting, my curiosity with the Black P-Stones grew. The Black P-Stones were a blood gang that frequented the apartment housing community known as *The Jungle*, located just east of La Brea Ave. and Coliseum St.

Unknowingly, most people thought this area was called, *The Jungle* because of the bestial crimes that sometime occur in this area. The name was established back in the sixties when elderly Jewish citizens occupied this area. Back then, as it is now, large palm trees and swimming pools resembling a tropical jungle shaded the area.

Today, these large palm trees are not only used for shade, they are also used to conceal gang members while they snipe at rival gang members and police. Even though the residents themselves call their home, *The Jungle*, LAPD is forbidden to use the term because the City Council ruled the term derogatory toward Black people. LAPD referred to it as Lower Baldwin Hills.

Although I grew up just thirty seconds away, I never once stepped foot in *The Jungle* before becoming a police officer. As a youth, the rule of thumb was, never go into *The*

196

Jungle or to the Baldwin Hills Movie Theater because blood gang members ruled them both. That's one of the reasons why I jumped at the opportunity to work off-duty at the Baldwin Hills Movie Theater even though it was for lower pay than most off-duty jobs. I wanted to help erase the negative stereotype that I once had for the theater.

On the corner of Nicolet Ave. and Coco Ave. I saw three gang members walking in our direction. A red danger light flashed in my head. Something wasn't right. Usually, whenever the police drove up, the gang members would either run or start walking in the opposite direction. This time, they not only continued to walk in the direction of the patrol car, but they casually drank from forty ounce bottles of Old English 800. As they continued to walk toward the car, my heart began to pound and my throat began to get dry. I unfastened my seat belt in anticipation of a confrontation. I looked over at my partner to see what his reaction was. He seemed unconcerned. My partner continued to look down and thumb through his calendar date book.

What's wrong with this old joker? Can't he see them coming? The bloods walked directly to my partner's window. "What's up dog?" they asked him.

"Dog? Why are they calling you their dog?" I asked my partner.

"Because a dog is man's best friend. It's a positive term," he explained.

Extending his hand, my partner replied, "Hey, how *yawl* doing?"

The bloods switched their forty ounce bottles of beer from their right hand into their left hand and formed a greeting

197

line to shake my partner's hand. As they exchanged greetings, my partner with concern, asked each one of them about the well being of their mothers and older brothers by name.

"Where is Fat Rat?" he asked. "Tell him that I want to see him."

My new partner was like the Sheriff Andy Taylor of *The Jungle*. He knew everybody and his mama and they all loved him. I formed the opinion that if he was Sheriff Andy Taylor then I was like Deputy Barney Fife because no one liked me.

Thump! I suddenly felt the patrol car bounce up and down. Looking back in the rear view mirror, I saw a forth gang member sitting on the trunk of the car drinking a forty ounce.

"Forget that crap! Enough is enough!" I shouted out loud. Busting out of the car door, I screamed, "Get your fat butt off the car!"

Everyone including my partner froze with his mouth open. I was in a rage.

"Pour it out. Pour it out." I repeatedly shouted.

Drinking in public was like a major felony to me. I walked up to the gang member nearest me and snatched the beer bottle out of his hand. I then poured its contents out on the ground. It was cold too! I frantically walked around in a circle yelling like a raving mad dog.

"Yo dog, what's up with your boy? Why is he trippin? We ain't hurtin nobody," one asked. Then like a little boy whining to his father, the blood asked my partner, "Do we really have to pour out the beer?"

My partner calmly stepped out of the car. Like a father explaining the facts of life to his children, he calmly said, "Everyone does police work differently. I don't care if you

198

drink as long as you're not disturbing anybody but that's just me. If my partner wants you to pour your beer out then you're going to have to do it."

Like pouting little children, the gang members stubbornly poured out their beer and walked away cursing me under their breath.

"Yeah, back at you!" I shouted.

Taking a closer look at me, one of the gang members replied, "Aw, it's you. You're the one that got me locked up six months ago!"

"You got yourself locked up!"

"Naw, blood! You da one dat came to court and lied to the judge!"

"I didn't lie to anybody."

"Yeah you did. My attorney asked you how I got the bruise on my face and you said it was there when you arrested me."

"Oh, that lie? Wasn't it there before?"

"Hell naw blood! You know I got it when you kicked me in the face. That was messed up blood! You didn't hafta kick me in my face like dat!"

"If you run from the police and get caught, what do you expect to happen? We're not here to play games. This ain't freeze tag where we touch you and you freeze. If you run and get caught, you pay the price. It's not my fault that you're slow and can't fight!"

"I ain't slow! The only reason you caught me was because I was on sherm that night. If I hadn't been smoking PCP you wouldn't have caught me."

199

"I can catch you anytime. I could have caught you if you were on steroids," I told him.

"Take your gun and badge off and we can go head up now!"

"Go get a job and just say no sometimes, shermhead!"

My partner interrupted me, "Hey partner, whatever you want to do is fine with me but if I may ask, why does drinking in public make you so angry?"

Taking a deep breath and exhaling, I thought about it for a second. No one had ever asked me that question before. Everyone just assumed everything I did was out of hatred toward gang members but the reasons for all of my actions were deeper than that.

Answering my partner's question, I said, "It's a long story. I hate alcoholics." I left the conversation at that because I trusted my partner with my life but not with my life story.

"Have you ever thought about being more friendly toward gang members? They aren't that bad," he said.

Why would I want to be friendly with any other gang members?

Every year since the age of thirteen I ate Thanksgiving and Christmas dinner next to a Rollin Sixties crip. My cousin Ray was the only gang member who I needed to be friendly with. I had no love for the rest!

"Hey, do you mind if we go and get some soul food for lunch?" my partner asked.

"That's fine with me but I don't eat that stuff."

"What? You're not a real Black man if you don't eat soul food."

200

I couldn't believe he said that. *Not this again!* I thought to myself.

"How can Black people condemn White people for making jokes about the way some Black people talk and what they eat when Black people put each other down for not conforming to the stereotypes?" I asked.

I was already steamed. My partner's remarks just added fuel to the fire. "Being Black is not what you eat. I guess you have to drink forty ounces to be Black, *huh*?"

"Take it easy. I was just kidding. Seriously, why don't you eat soul food? Where your parents from?" He curiously asked.

"My mother is from Texas and my father's from Arkansas. I don't eat soul food because that's slavery food. That's the slave masters' leftovers. Besides, that greasy stuff is bad for you."

"So what do you eat then?"

"I'm a free Black man so I eat chili cheese dogs, chili cheese fries and double chili cheese burgers, my brotha."

"You've got problems son."

Within a short time, my partner and I became good friends. My partner playfully called me his son because every time I went berserk on a gang member they would complain to him as if he was my father.

It was interesting to see him do police work. Working with him gave me a chance to meet and talk to gang members who would normally run when I drove up. He showed me a different way of doing things. He never sweated anyone for information. All he had to do was put out the word that he wanted to know something and there would be at least two or

201

three messages waiting for him at the station with the information he wanted.

Although I enjoyed working with my partner, I quickly grew to hate PM watch. There was too much traffic, too many people on the street, and too many domestic dispute calls to answer.

Every time I went to a family dispute I made it a point to always arrest someone. Sometimes I'd arrest both the male and female for something. I felt both were to blame because no one really knew just how much psychological damage a child received by watching his parents abuse one another.

As a child my cousin Ray would run over to my house at least once a week excited. Ray lived just six blocks and another world away from me. My cousin was practically raised by my mother because his parents were going through a physically violent divorce.

"Guess what?" he would say. "Last night my mother tried to stab my daddy in the neck. He got mad and punched her in the jaw and knocked her out. You missed it!"

One night before our little league championship game Ray climbed out of his bedroom window and disappeared after his mother and father had a huge fight. Ray was the star third baseman and clean up hitter. He never showed up to the game and we lost. That game meant a lot to me. Because of Ray's absence, I was moved from starting pitcher to third base where I dropped the game-winning hit. Ray would have caught it. Now, I was more than determined not to ever drop the ball on domestic violence plays.

Back then, I was envious of him because he seemed to always have more fun and excitement in his life than I did. I was now mad because I knew all that fun and excitement greatly contributed to my cousin's present situation. Maybe if one of his parents would have went to jail, he might not have turned out the way he did, in prison.

I never lost any sleep over a domestic violence arrest. I once arrested a feeble seventy-five year old man for pushing his wife onto a bed. The woman sustained a minor laceration and a knot on her head from hitting the bedpost. My partner was totally unconcerned about the incident.

"Let's get the hell out of here!" he said. "This old man can't hurt anybody. Even if he does hurt her, I'm sure that she is use to it by now. She's probably been getting her butt kicked for fifteen years."

The LAPD manual said if a police officer observed any visible injuries on a spouse, the officer had no choice but to arrest the suspect. Going against my partner's wishes, I arrested the old man for spousal battery, which was a felony. He was booked and placed in the felony cell with robbers and burglars. His fifty thousand dollar bail was double that of his cell mates. Many of my coworkers said I was cold hearted.

On another occasion I responded to a domestic violence call in the Lower Baldwin Hills area. A young Black woman in her late twenties opened the front door. Peeping through the security bar doors, I could see blood dripping from a cut on her forehead. Blood was also sprouting from a puncture wound in the woman's shoulder. The sight of the injuries caused me to predetermine that her spouse was going to jail.

"What in the world do *ya'll* want? We didn't call no police!" the woman impolitely shouted.

Once we got inside the apartment, I saw her husband casually sitting on the couch bleeding from his leg, hand and stomach. Blood was grotesquely splattered on all four walls. I was really surprised to learn neither one of them phoned the police or fire department for assistance.

A neighbor who heard the two screaming at each other generated the 911 call. My partner and I interviewed both suspects separately. Like children, they persistently blamed the other. Both claimed they acted in self-defense. My partner, like most officers, elected to arrest only the husband. Through intense bickering, I persuaded my partner to allow me the satisfaction of arresting them both. The most disturbing part of the incident was their seven-year-old son watched the bloody confrontation. The trembling child was placed in the care of a relative until one of his parents could be released from jail. That made my day!

THE WONDER YEARS

"Even some police officers have a hard time standing up to these criminals. Most officers entering the Academy today are college graduates from stable backgrounds although they come from all socio-economic levels."

Former LAPD chief Daryl Gates regarding gang members. ("My life in the LAPD, Chief Daryl F. Gates" July 1992)

My father was a sanitation worker. He worked two full-time jobs so he could move his family from the troubled South Central Los Angeles neighborhood of 65th St. and Budlong Ave. into the beautiful confines of Windsor Hills. Windsor Hills was a two square mile area made up of large modern homes. The residents consisted of mostly doctors, attorneys, professional athletes and other professional people. Although this area was located close to the west side of Los Angeles, the media still referred to it as South Central LA if a news worthy crime occurred.

This often made the residents angry because they didn't want to be stereotyped with *the hood*. They would never say *da hood*. The middle class Black neighborhood, which sat high above the inner city, gave its residents the false security they had been liberated from the crime and violence that took place below.

Despite my father functioning on only four hours of sleep, he still found the time to coach my little league baseball team when all my other friend's fathers wouldn't. He also found time to whip my tail when I needed it. My mother didn't have the time to work. She raised eight children and several grandchildren.

Being born the last of eight children created an unusual situation for me. At the time of my birth, three of my older brothers and sisters were in their thirties with families of their own. I was already an uncle five times over at birth.

My family was not without problems. For reasons unknown to me, my oldest brother and sister were both functional alcoholics. My brother, a successful businessman, would return home every evening from business dinners drunk. He would then have a few more drinks to help him wind down from his stressful day. Frustrated and enraged, his wife would often phone my mother and express a need for a better life.

My second oldest sister was a divorced single mother of three. Every night she would drink herself comatose. When I was about six years old, I vividly remembered being awakened late one night by a phone call from my sister's children. Crying hysterically, they told my mother they were unable to wake their mother, fearing she was dead. Still wearing pajamas, sleepy eyed and confused, my mother and I made a trek across town to my sister's house near Central Ave and 33rd St., the east side of town. As we drove east on Jefferson Blvd, I used landmarks to judge our proximity. The towering, bright red lighthouse shaped brick buildings forming the U.S.C campus meant we were getting close to our destination. Crossing the railroad tracks meant we were half way there. The dark, dirty old junkyard signified we were just around the corner from my sister's house.

206

I was still half asleep when we arrived. As I walked through the door, the strong piercing smell of alcohol, cigarettes and vomit burned my nostrils. Like smelling salt reviving a dazed boxer, I was immediately knocked to my senses.

"Yuck! It stinks in here," I said.

I bent over and grabbed my stomach. I then opened up my mouth and let out a loud groan as if I was going to throw up. My mother slapped me on the head and ordered me into the house. Stepping over clothes and beer bottles, I gingerly made my way into the house. I then saw my oldest sister lying motionless on the living room couch with her mouth wide open. An empty bottle of Jack Daniel's was resting on the floor underneath her out stretched arm.

"Dang! Is she dead?" I asked.

"No, she is just drunk," my mother replied.

"She looks dead to me."

My mother, who was a devoted Christian woman, despairingly fell to her knees and broke down in tears.

Clamping her hands together and pleading with God, she asked, "Please Lord, help my daughter overcome this sickness."

I had never seen my mother cry before. As I watched her cry, I began to feel sad for her. I too began to cry. I tried to console her by putting my arms around her. While the tears rolled down my face, I said, "I promise mother, I will never get drunk for as long as I live."

It was then that I saw firsthand how alcoholism not only destroyed the user but how it broke down everyone who cared for that person. Every night before going to bed, I would kneel down and pray for God to heal my two lost siblings. Two years later, my sister miraculously stopped drinking and became a born again Christian. She devoted every day of her life to helping her church and a multitude of underprivileged children and adults. Her recovery strongly developed my faith in prayer and at an early age, it gave me the confidence that I, along with God, could change the world.

Three of my other older siblings were very much involved in the Black Power movement of the early seventies. All three barely fell short of being directly involved with the Black Panther Party. They actively took part in demonstrations on their college campuses.

"Power to the people," is what I would shout while raising my fist in the air. As a young impressionable kid, I very much wanted to be a Black Panther mainly because I thought they looked cool wearing black leather coats and black berets. I didn't fully understand the meaning of their fight and struggle because I also wanted to be a *pig*. There was no way a person could be pro-panther and pro *pig*. Back then, police officers and cops were not in my vocabulary. A police officer was always referred to as a *pig*.

My brother sported a huge afro, sideburns, a full-length black leather coat, dark shades and a black brief case. As a result, the *pigs* would stop him every morning on his way to school. Their daily routine consisted of searching his pockets and car for weapons. Their probable cause for stopping him was simply based on the way he looked.

One of my sisters was so into the movement she changed her birth name and adopted a Swahili name. I was given a charcoal black colored dog named Zuri as a gift for my seventh birthday. Zuri meant beautiful in Swahili.

By the time I was ten years old, I had thumbed through so called Black revolutionary books such as the autobiographies of Malcolm X, Angela Davis, and Ice Berg Slim. I read the Autobiography of Malcolm X in its entirety in the 5th grade; long before Spike Lee's movie "X" made it popular to do so. Many times, I intently listened to my brother and sisters talk about how all Black people had a responsibility to help one another succeed.

By the age of ten, I had developed into a Black conscious militant who thought I was going to grow up and change the world. I knew whatever profession I chose, it would involve helping minorities rise above racial oppression.

When I was eight years old, my grandmother became ill and was confined to a wheelchair. Every Saturday, my mother would drop Ray and me off at my oldest sister's house while she ran errands for my grandmother. Full of energy, we would get on our bicycles and vigorously pedal down the smelly, garbage filled alleys, skillfully maneuvering around fallen winos on our way to the warehouse loading docks on Central Avenue. Once there, we would wait until the coast was clear. Then, we'd sneak inside the warehouse and steal bags of potato chips and sodas. After our mission was completed, we would ride home and marvel at our feat.

Two years later, my grandmother passed away. Ray and I began to spend more time at his house because his mother gave us a lot more leeway to roam the streets than my mother would allow. As time went on, our fascination with crime continued to grow into full-scale shoplifting excursions. I

209

would divert the store clerk's attention while Ray stuffed his pockets with anything he could get.

My youthful criminal activity continued for several months until I was caught by a security guard while on a solo venture. Terrified and sobbing, I begged the guard not to tell my father. My father was a quiet and soft-spoken man, but when he got angry, he could easily have been the meanest man alive. Stories of his unmerciful child beatings circulated through my family like old horror tales. I feared nothing more than my father's belt.

Desperately begging and pleading, I said, "Please don't tell my father. You don't understand. He is going to kill me."

The guard just looked at me and laughed. Ten minutes later I heard footsteps coming down the hall. Suddenly, the door flew open with such force it slammed back against the wall. Pictures rattled and papers blew off the security guard's desk. There my father stood, stoned faced with veins bulging from his forehead. His presence was painful. Without saying a word he produced terror in my heart and the security guard's as well. On my way out the door, the security guard grabbed me by my arm.

"You are right. Your dad is going to kill you, sorry," he said.

Oh, gee thanks. Him feeling sorry for me isn't going to help my cause one bit!

Forty inches long, one and a half inches wide, black leather; it was the belt from hell. The first blow struck me on the back of my legs with such force my knees buckled. As I lay on the ground in a fetal position, my dear old dad delivered

210

smashing blows all over my head and body. Sweating profusely and grunting loudly with each swing, my father continued to beat me like a runaway slave until all his energy was drained. He looked disappointed when he had to quit. He probably regretted not pacing himself. Fortunately for him, this incident took place in the summertime when school was out. If it hadn't, the Department of Children's Services would have surely paid him a visit and demanded an explanation for the bruises on my arms and face.

Today I am thankful that I had a father who cared enough to discipline me. That memorable butt whipping was like the book "Dianetics," which promises to positively change the reader's life forever. My much-deserved whipping did change my life forever. For some, the only butt whipping they will ever receive will be from the police. By then the beating will be too late and possibly too severe to have a positive affect on their lives.

Consequently, my curiosity with crime came to an abrupt end. However, where mine ended, Ray's was just beginning. His theft escalated into burglary. Three years later he was arrested and convicted of multiple counts of burglary. Among the items stolen were several guns. Because of the severity, Ray was subsequently sentenced to eighteen months in the California Youth Authority.

LOCK DOWN

"There is going to be a massacre in the future and they know that. There is the Rolling '60s group. They went into a sporting goods store and stole 50 Uzis, 3,000 rounds (of ammunition) . . ."

Former LAPD Detective Mark Fuhrman. (Based on transcripts used by the O.J Simpson defense lawyers)

I received news from Ray's father that Ray had been transferred from a Northern California institution to a state prison near the city of San Diego. It had been two years since I'd seen Ray. After letting the hair on my head and face grow, Ray's father and I anxiously made a two-hour trip to visit Ray. This would not be the first time I had visited my cousin in a correctional facility but it would be my first visit to a state prison as a police officer. My cousin had been incarcerated off and on since the young innocent age of fifteen. His thirty-two-page rap sheet hosted an assortment of felony crimes and convictions. These convictions and arrests were real unlike the ones I had made on him when we were children playing "cops and robbers."

While on the freeway, memories of my first visit to a correction facility were still fresh in my mind. It was as if it was yesterday. I will never forget how Ray's mother neatly packed Ray's father, his little brother, Dee, and I, a picnic basket filled with sandwiches, fruit, and sodas. Unlike normal families, we were not going camping nor were we going picnicking at a park. The broken family was on their way to visit Ray up in the mountains at the California Youth Authority. The drive seemed to last forever as we drove up a narrow and endlessly winding snow covered mountain road. Finally, we came to a high chain link fence with a small wooden guard shack in front of it. Behind the fence I could see what appeared to be a large grassy field lined with lunch benches.

"We are here!" Ray's father excitedly yelled.

"This is it? This is C.Y.A.?" I disappointedly asked.

I was totally baffled. There were no guard towers with killer snipers watching and waiting to shoot fleeing inmates, nor were there any guards patrolling the perimeter with vicious German shepherds. I was expecting to see something resembling a Nazi prison camp.

While Ray's father checked us in, Dee and I cleared snow off a lunch bench and took a seat. Five minutes later, Ray came chugging through the snow. Excited, Ray told us stories about the fun he was having. Every morning he had to wake up at 5:00 a.m. and clear debris from fire trails. He said he had aspirations of becoming a fire fighter someday. As he continued to speak with vigor, I became more and more disgusted with the thought of him having so much fun. I was always envious of Ray because he could stay out all night and do almost whatever he pleased. I was also jealous because I got my butt whipped for stealing a pack of gum while he got rewarded with YMCA camp for committing a felony.

EVEN THOUGH OUR LIFE STYLES WERE CONSIDERABLY DIFFERENT, we still managed to stay in touch and be there for one another during memorable time periods in our lives.

One day I came home from school and my mother told me Ray was home from C.Y.A. I immediately, jumped on my bicycle and furiously peddled to Ray's house. Rounding the street corner, I saw about twelve guys standing in front of Ray's house. Judging by their attire, there wasn't any question these guys were all gang members, no doubt his new friends. As I pulled up on the grass and exited off my bike, I was greeted with evil stares and defensive stands. Ray stepped out of the group and greeted me with a smile and a handshake. We were happy to see each other.

"What's up?" I asked.

"Nothing. What's up with you?"

"Nothing. What you doing?"

"Nothing. What you doing?"

I had so much to ask Ray but I didn't know where to start. A couple of weeks after Ray's return, his mother went out of town for the weekend. My mother insisted he stay with us so he wouldn't get into trouble while his mother was gone. During the day Ray walked home and hung out with his homeboys. At night, he returned to my house. Every night we would lie in our beds with the lights off and talk about life. By now Ray had been kicked out of four high schools mainly for poor attendance.

The first high school he was kicked out of was Palisades High, which was located in the filthy rich area of Palisades and twenty-five miles from his home. By choice, he was bused there because his mother thought the rich White atmosphere would be good for him. Ray had to get up every morning at 5:00 a.m. to catch the school bus. If he missed the school bus he would have to catch four public buses to get

214

there. By the time he arrived, school would almost be over. The second school was Westchester High School which was located in a middle-class White area. This school was only fifteen miles from his home. From there Ray went far to the east side of town to attend Jefferson High School. When that fell through, he finally rested at Crenshaw High school. The "Shaw" was widely known for its nationally ranked basketball team and its high enrollment of "neighborhood" crips.

I was curious as to why he stopped going to school, especially since Ray's grades were always higher than mine.

"How come you never go to school?" I asked.

"I go to school everyday. I just don't go to class."

"Why not? You're not dumb. In junior high you got way better grades than I did. What happened to you?"

"I don't really know," he said. "I got kicked out of Palisades High because I couldn't wake up in time to catch the school bus. A couple of times I caught the R.T.D bus to school but by the time I got there, school was half way over.

After I got kicked out, my mother made me go live with my father on the east side, which didn't make sense. If you want a child to improve, you do not send him to a rival gang infested school on the east side. The first time I shot someone was on my way home from Jefferson High School."

Several of Ray's friends had told me he was going around shooting people but I never could figure out how much was factual and how much was exaggerated rumors. Now, I was actually hearing it from the horse's mouth.

"Really?" I asked with amazement. "Tell me what happened?"

215

"I was taking a short cut home through an alley and some fool came at me wrong so I blasted him."

"Did he die?" I had to ask.

"I don't know. I never went back down that alley and I never saw him again. I know that I hit him because I saw blood on his shirt."

"Damn, that's deep! Do you think that you'll ever get out of this gang stuff?"

"Probably not. I don't know anybody that has. Most likely I will go to prison for murder or get killed."

We continued to talk for hours until my mother pounded on the door. "Shut up and go to sleep! It's three thirty in the morning!"

AT THE AGE OF SEVENTEEN RAY WAS ARRESTED in conjunction with several robberies and placed in the Los Angeles County Jail to be tried as an adult. Once again his father and I were off to see my little incarcerated cousin. It had been a while since I'd seen Ray. At that time most of our contacts had been made by phone because I felt uncomfortable going over to Ray's house. Every time I went over there I was greeted by hostile gang members or hostile Lennox Sheriffs who routinely patrolled by his house. Since we resembled one another, there was always the possibility of me getting shot by one of Ray's enemies as a result of mistaken identity.

Rival gang members didn't care if they shot a non-gang affiliated person. If a kid was between the ages of thirteen and twenty-one and was caught walking near a known

216

gang hangout, they automatically qualified for a bullet in the head. No questions asked.

As soon as I walked into the county jail reception center, a young White deputy standing at the front door visually scanned visitors for weapons. The deputy grabbed me by my arm.

"Hey little hommie, come here!" the deputy said in a stern voice.

He couldn't be talking to me.

Looking at the deputy as if he were crazy, I pointed to myself and asked, "Who me?"

Irritated, the deputy replied, "Yeah you! Are you stupid or something? Who else would I be talking to? Do you have any guns or knives on you?"

"Who me?"

The deputy quickly ran his hand across my upper body. He then went down and squeezed my groin area.

Flinching, I yelled, "Hey, watch it!"

The deputy pointed his finger in my face and said, "You better not start any trouble in here! Do you understand me?"

"Who me?"

I was furious. I felt violated. It was as though the deputy was getting some kind of sexual gratification from the frisk.

"How come he searched me and nobody else?" I asked Ray's father who was laughing.

"He must have thought you were a crip because you are wearing blue pants and a blue shirt."

217

"Cops are so stupid! They think that every Black person who is wearing blue or red is in a gang. If I would have been White I bet they wouldn't have done that."

"Relax. He was just trying to do his job. I guess they have a lot of problems with gangs in here," Ray's father replied.

TEN YEARS LATER I VISITED HIM AGAIN AT THE COUNTY JAIL. This time, I was an off-duty police officer. Upon arriving at the county jail, the first thing I did was walk up to a tall, dorky, blonde female deputy and identified myself as a police officer. I asked the deputy if she wanted me to check my gun in before I entered the building. The deputy turned toward a sergeant standing at the other end of the crowded room and yelled, "Hey Sergeant!" Pointing at me, she said, "I have an off-duty LAPD officer here that wants to visit an inmate. What do you want me to do with his gun?"

As if E.F. Hutton had just spoken, the room was so quiet you could hear a pin drop. Everyone's attention was turned in my direction.

"Aw let him keep it. He won't come in physical contact with the inmates anyway."

With a serious look on her face, the deputy leaned toward me and whispered, "Go ahead and keep your gun. Besides, you never know who might recognize you as a police officer in here. The people visiting in here don't like the police because that's who put their relatives in here."

"Duuuuh," I looked at the deputy in disbelief. I thought LAPD was the only agency that hired morons. Eighteen months later, Ray was released.

UNDERNEATH MY EAGERNESS TO SEE RAY WAS
A DEEP FEAR. I wondered if this prison tour had changed the
way he viewed my job and me. I also worried about the
possibility of seeing an inmate whom I had put there. I didn't
want anyone to vindicate his or her anger on Ray. As we
exited from the highway onto a small paved road, in the
distance, I could see several guard towers peering over the
rural hilly terrain.

Once inside the prison grounds, we had to take a bus
to Ray's compound. From there we had to stand in a long line
and wait to see if our names had been approved. To get to the
visitation center we had to pass through two electronically
operated metal doors, a guard tower, and two twenty-foot high
barbed wire gates. Lastly, we had to walk through two more
metal doors. This time my visit to a prison was everything I
had imagined it would be. I saw plenty of high walls, guard
towers, and barbed wire fences. In a sick and demented way, I
was sort of proud of Ray because he had finally reached this
plateau. I was sad because I wanted to believe this was the
ambition of the old Ray. The new Ray wanted to be a father
and a model citizen.

As I nervously walked into the center, I felt out of
place. I felt as though I was wearing my blue LAPD uniform. I
wondered if any of the inmates sensed my
uneasiness. Judging by the guard's evil stares, I could tell they
didn't know I was a police officer. To them I was just another
future resident. I didn't expect the visitation center to be so
deep inside the prison.

Standing at the door, I scanned the room and checked
for any and all possible escape routes. There were none. The

last thing I wanted to do was become a hostage during a prison riot. Finally, I picked a table closest to the metal door. As I walked by each little round, brown wooden table, I looked down at each one to see if I knew any of the inmates. Thank God I didn't!

Fifteen minutes later Ray entered through a door at the back of the room. He looked different. His hair was braided in corn rolls. Each braid was held together by a blue rubber band. Now, for the first time, he really looked like a dangerous criminal.

As usual, he was in good spirits. He seemed to be enjoying his new home. "Oh. I've seen a couple people in here that you know." Ray said.

He then began talking about the people he's seen as if I had missed a big party. For hours we talked about old times and old friends we had come across in our lives. Our main topic consisted of swapping war stories and bagging on each other.

"Damn, you look crazy. What happened to all your hair?" he asked.

"No. You look crazy with those long braids," I responded.

"You look like a Black skin head."

"You look like a Black Charles Manson," I came back.

"So how's work? Have you shot anybody yet?" he asked.

"Nope but if things keep up the way they've been going, it won't be long. I come close to shooting someone every night. Speaking of shooting, I ran into one of your homeboys the other night. Do you know someone named Bone?" I asked.

"Yeah, I know a Big Bone, a Baby Bone and a Little Bone."

"This was Big Bone. Last week I caught him creepin through Thirties hood. He saw us and tried to lose us by speeding through some alleys. After we caught him we impounded his car because he didn't have a driver's license. He had a cast on his leg and he was on crutches. My partner wanted to make him walk on crutches to a payphone. He was hoping that he would get shot on the way. I insisted that we drop him off at the nearest payphone which we did."

"He probably tossed a gun out of the car when he went down the alley," Ray said. "I've done that many of times."

My feelings toward Ray were conflicting. I was sad to see my relative incarcerated but in my heart I knew my cousin belonged there. Ray never denied being a dangerous criminal and until recently, he never said he would change. While we were talking, an inmate came around and handed us a paper menu. Listed on the menu was an assortment of food dishes and entrees.

"How's the food taste?"

"It's okay."

"Where's it come from?"

"The kitchen."

"You mean it's prison food? I thought you guys ate bread and water?"

To my surprise the food was actually good. After grubbing down on convict food, we walked outside onto a small

221

patio surrounded by ten-foot cement walls. We then stylishly folded our arms and posed for a Polaroid picture. It was hard to look cheerful while taking a picture in a prison but I did the best I could. Once the picture was done, we again took our seats.

As I looked into Ray's face, I saw the frightening image of myself wearing prison blue instead of LAPD blue. My fear was warranted because I believed every police officer was only one bad day away from being incarcerated. All it took was for an officer to get caught up in a moment of excitement and deliver one blow too many to a suspect. This was something I had already been guilty of doing. In my short term as a police officer, I had seen a number of my coworkers sentenced to prison for felony crimes committed on and off-duty.

Trying not to stare, I looked around the room at each inmate and wondered what they were in for. Watching the inmates interact felt weird because I was use to seeing them on the streets when they were hostile and angry. I carefully watched each one of them lovingly interact with their families, especially with their children. Buffed out men were clutching their children, wives, mothers and girlfriends as though they really cared for them. I couldn't help noticing a few tears of remorse excreting from several inmates' eyes as they appeared to long for their families. I figured if an inmate was really concerned about his family he wouldn't embarrass them by committing a crime. One inmate romantically gazed in his woman's eyes and held her hand the whole two hours I was there. Others played dominoes and card games with their visitors. Every one of them seemed like the perfect family man who had been rehabilitated by the system. I knew better.

I bet the only time these knuckle heads spend time with their families is when they are locked up and can't hang out with the homies! I said to myself.

"Hey fool! Stop staring at people. Somebody is going to think something is wrong with you," Ray whispered.

"Sorry, I can't help it. Some of these guys look crazy," I responded.

Still looking around, I said to myself, *so this is what I do.*

Very few police officers ever get a chance to see the finished product of their arrest. Being a police officer is like working at an automotive plant and having never seen a car on the road. All police officers ever know is if the defendant is found either guilty or innocent. If it wasn't for police officers having to keep track of their overtime hours, they wouldn't even know that.

It was weird! I started off as a cocky young man who wanted to make a change. Somehow I evolved into the very problem I was trying to solve. What happened to me and what was the turning point? Ironically, I was sitting inside of a prison reflecting on my life and career.

LAPD ACADEMY

November 3, 1989 at 6:30 a.m., I stood at attention in the LAPD Academy gymnasium. My knees were shaking. I was clean-shaven and dressed in a dark blue suit. As I nervously looked around the gym, the first thing I noticed was there were only twelve Black recruits. Somehow, thousands of Black applicants had been eliminated during the selection process.

What in the hell did I get myself into?

My drill instructor was a tall, thin White officer in his late fifties. He looked exceptionally sharp in his long sleeve uniform, decorated with Navy ribbons, LAPD stripes and hash marks. I so was impressed!

I was not impressed with my physical training instructor. She was a short, mean Hispanic female officer. Scanning over the eighty-nine recruits, she somehow singled me out of the group.

Looking directly into my eyes, she yelled, "Recruit, you look like you have an attitude. There are enough people like you hanging out on the street!

224

Middle-class Black college graduates? I questioned to myself. *I don't think so!*

"We don't need any in here! I'm going to personally see to it that you don't graduate from here!" she continued. "I hope you still have the number to your old job because you're going to need it mister!"

As I stood at a position of attention, ridged, eyes forward and arms locked down at my side, I couldn't help but envision myself handcuffed while sitting on a curb being verbally abused by a cop. A scene I saw almost every day. My natural instinct was to rebel.

Despite my physical training instructor's futile efforts to run me to death, the academy was relatively easy for me. I realized she was only doing her job by yelling in my face and trying to mold me into a police officer. This technique had a reverse affect on me as a recruit officer. In the back of my mind, I still viewed the police as a symbol of racism and repression in the Black community.

Someone else must have thought something similar to what I was feeling because shortly after the 1992 riot, a study of LAPD's training techniques was reviewed by retired US Superior Court Judge Warren Christopher. The whole structure of the police academy was subsequently changed from a hostile environment to a more relaxed college campus environment. Old timers believed this type of atmosphere generated weak-minded police officers. They also believed it enabled more women to slide through the system.

APRIL FIFTH WAS MY POLICE ACADEMY GRADUATION DAY. Six months of verbal abuse made it

225

seem like two years had passed. My family was more excited about graduation than I was. I probably would have quit if it weren't for the verbal abuse I had received from my physical training instructor. I also would have quit if it weren't for the fact that I had to prove to family and friends I could become a police officer. Early in the academy I learned that I didn't like the mentality of police officers any more now that I was about to become one than when I was a teenager. Ninety-five percent of my academy classmates were recruit jerks, training to be patrol jerks.

The only thing that kept me going was my gun and badge. During the third week, my classmates and I received our LAPD identification card and badge with the sole purpose of taking the badge home to polish it for daily inspections. A LAPD badge and identification card was like having a "L.A. Express card," a police officer could get into almost any club in Southern California free of charge or half price. Since my physical training instructor vowed to get rid of me, I decided to take full advantage of my benefits while they lasted.

Teaming up with one of my classmates, recruit officer Green from Sacramento, every night we'd hit a different club. Thursday night was our favorite night to party. Every Thursday night without exception, we would go to a club in Hollywood called Paradise 24. As police officers, we got VIP treatment, avoiding the long lines and high cost. Nobody knew we were only unarmed recruits still in the academy. After partying until three in the morning, I would only get two hours of sleep before going to the academy. Once there I would summon the strength to run five miles and do an unforgivable amount of pushups in the heat.

226

I remember one particular time I went out to a club in West Covina called the Safari Bar. Flashing my badge to the bouncer, I coolly strolled passed the long line outside the club. The bouncer grabbed me by my arm and shouted something in my ear. The loud thumping music drowned him out. The bouncer then escorted me inside the club and directed me to a crowded table. Sitting at the table was the whole academy physical training staff.

Shocked, a sharp, knifing pain stabbed me in my chest as I saw my physical training instructor's mouth drop open. Lowering my head, I made a quick turn and headed out the back exit. I was hoping she might think she was seeing things.

The next day my class went on a grueling ten mile run up hills in the scorching heat. Several of my classmates passed out from exhaustion. Tired and bewildered, my classmates tried to figure out why our physical training instructor was so angry with us. She never said a word about it. Acting puzzled, I never said a word either but I knew why.

SEARCHING THROUGH THE CROWD, I SPOTTED MY COUSIN RAY SITTING NEXT TO MY MOTHER. My cousin Ray was an admitted gang member and an ex-convict who hated the police. Almost more surprising than seeing him on LAPD academy grounds, was the fact that he was actually wearing a dress shirt, slacks and a hat to cover his shoulder length braids.

Without question, I was surprised to see him. One night while partying at a club, I ran into one of Ray's friends who told me the LAPD in conjunction with the Los Angeles

227

County Sheriffs Department, had unsuccessfully served two felony robbery warrants at Ray's mother's house. I couldn't believe one of LAPD's most wanted criminals would have the nerve to calmly sit on LAPD's most sacred ground.

What nerve! Criminals just don't care!

After the ceremony, I told my cousin I couldn't believe he showed up.

"Damn, I can't believe I came up here either but I had to see this for myself. I can't believe you actually went through with it." Ray said laughing.

Suddenly, Ray stopped laughing and looked extremely nervous. Just then I felt a hand on my newly ordained shoulder. Thinking it was a family member I turned around with a smile. Snapping into a position of attention, I saw controversial Police Chief Daryl Gates standing in front of me with his hand extended.

Shaking my hand, Chief Gates said, "Congratulations officer. I know you will make a fine police officer someday." He then extended his had to Ray and said, "I know you're proud of your brother."

As Ray politely shook the chief's hand, he smiled and then shook his head up and down. The chief then continued to make his way through the crowd shaking hands with the new officers and their families.

Ray pounded his fist into his hand and angrily said, "Damn, I should have shot that prejudice cop!"

Very few Black Los Angeles residents held a high regard for the chief. Many felt he was prejudice against all minorities, especially Black people. A couple of years prior he made a public statement and implied Black people had a higher rate of death from the police chokehold because they were abnormal.

Ray again smiled and said, "Promise me that you won't tell any of my friends that I shook his hand. It would be bad for my reputation."

As he requested, I didn't tell anyone. Despite him acting angry and hostile toward the Chief of police, I knew deep down inside he felt a little honored and privileged to shake the hand of the most recognized person in Los Angeles. How many wanted gang members can say they met the chief, period?

A few minutes later, my smiling physical training instructor approached us. "I am so proud of you! You really did an excellent job. You took everything we dished out to you."

"Who me?"

Extending her hand, she said, "You can call me by my first name if you want."

Snarling, I replied, "No thanks, but now you can call me officer!"

Humiliated and angered, she responded, "You know what? You're a jerk!"

I hadn't stepped off the academy grounds as a police officer and yet I was already being called a jerk. I was shocked by my instructor's response. How else did she expect me to respond after calling me worthless, making me do extra sit-ups and humiliating me in front of my classmates. Maybe she did like me and was proud I was able to withstand her verbal abuse but who cared! She put me through hell.

GANG TRAINING

A couple of months after my graduation from the LAPD academy, I went over to my cousin's house for a brief visit. I pushed open Ray's bedroom door with authority and proudly strolled into the room with my sixteen round, nine millimeter, semi-automatic handgun holstered on my hip. I may not have been happy with the job, but I still loved the power and authority the badge and gun represented. Rising out of bed, Ray looked down at my side and smiled.

Sensing that I was feeling proud and cocky, Ray asked, "Is that the gun you carry on-duty?"

Grinning from ear to ear, I patted my holster and replied, "Yep, this is my baby."

"Aw, that's such a cute little gun."

Ray then reached underneath his bed and pulled out a fully loaded AK-47 assault rifle with a thirty-round magazine.

"This is what Rolling Sixties crips carry on-duty!"

Ray again reached underneath his bed. This time he pulled out two Tac 9, thirty-five round automatic handguns.

"This is what I carry when I'm off-duty, just hanging out at the mall."

My mind was blown. I felt small, insignificant and inferior. It wasn't fair. Ray's guns were bigger than mine and I was the good guy.

"So what. But can you shoot straight?" I asked.

"Yeah. Remember Mack?" he replied.

Mack was one of his gang banging buddies who chose to go into the Marines rather than go to jail.

Ray continued, "Mack took me out to the desert and taught me how to shoot and clean my guns. I can get you one for cheap, if you want. Every cop should have at least one of these."

It sounded tempting but I had to decline. I also declined my cousin's invitation to hold the guns. The last thing I needed was a murder rap. We talked for hours. It seemed like the elements which once separated us years ago were now bridging the gap. I discovered we had something in common. During Ray's rookie years as a car thief, he stole at least three cars a week from the West Los Angeles Division area where I was a rookie officer. Ray gave me some valuable insight on a criminal's mindset.

"Always trust your instincts. Don't rely on the police computer to tell you that something is wrong," Ray said.

Dressing like a UCLA student, wearing a backpack and carrying a school notebook, Ray confessed he would smile and wave at passing police officers as he hot-wired cars near the UCLA campus. It was he who strongly opposed my decision to transfer to Southwest Division because he said, "The ghetto brings out the worst in people!"

Ironically, we started spending a lot of time together. Ray even started going to church with me on Sunday mornings. One night Ray called me on the phone.

"Guess what?"

"What?" I asked.

"My girlfriend is pregnant."

"That's great. Who is the father?" I asked.

231

"Me stupid!"

"To be honest, I never knew you had a girlfriend. You've been locked up for so long, I had my doubts. You know what I'm saying?" I replied.

"Shut up! That's what you cops always say. You guys think that's funny. Anyway, we've been seeing each other exclusively for a while now."

"So how do you feel about being a father?" I asked.

"It's cool. I wanna be around to raise my child. I want him to grow up in a healthy environment, not like the one I had. My child isn't going to see his parents yell, curse, argue and beat-up on each other. He's gonna be brought up right! First, I've got to clear up a couple of traffic warrants. I figure I'll do about six months and that's about it. I'll be out in plenty of time to see my child get born."

"That sounds like a good idea," I answered. "Since you're going back to jail, how about letting me buy some of your things from you?"

Like all potential convicts, everything Ray owned was for sale because he needed money to put on his jail books. The last time Ray went to prison, I bought his whole CD collection. This time, I bought his car stereo and amplifier for cheap. Against my better judgment, I went with Ray down to the Slauson Swap Meet to let one of his friends install my stereo. The Slauson Swap Meet was the official LA gang one stop shopping center. Hundreds of gang members from different *sets* shopped there on the weekends.

On the way down there, I asked Ray if he was carrying a gun. He replied, "No, I don't need one because I'm rolling with LAPD. You got my back."

232

The thought of it made my stomach hurt. While his friend installed my stereo, we sat on the metal railing outside the front door and watched the hoochies walk by. Suddenly, Ray nudged me and then pointed to a gray Oldsmobile Cutlass with two Jheri curled gang bangers inside. Like vultures, the car slowly circled around the parking lot.

Calmly, he said, "There's going to be some trouble. Those guys are East Coast crips. I recognize one of them from the pen."

The car came to a screeching stop in front of us. The driver pointed in our direction and yelled, "Them fools is Sixties! Blast *um*."

Ray, who was standing in front of me, took a step backwards and stood behind me crouching while holding on to the back of my shirt. Opening the door, the passenger began to step out of the car. I quickly lifted up my oversized shirt and unsnapped my holster. My heart began pounding a mile a minute. Before the passenger could exit out the door, the driver looked frantically around and grabbed him by the arm. He then whispered something in his ear. Suddenly, the driver sped off before the passenger could pull his leg back into the car and close the door.

Puzzled by their sudden departure, I asked Ray how come they didn't shoot. Looking at me as if I was joking, Ray said, "They probably didn't shoot because they knew you were the police. They probably thought that it was a set up."

I naively asked, "How could they have possibly known that I was a police officer?"

"Look at you. You look like a cop. You have a crew cut, no mustache, you are wearing tightly creased blue jeans

233

and a white T-shirt with an oversized shirt over it. Nobody dresses like that but fags and cops." Laughing, he said, "Maybe they left because they thought you were gay and you were going to bust their booties."

Angrily offended, I responded, "If they thought I was gay, it's because you were hiding behind me and holding onto me like a woman!"

"I was not hiding. I was letting you do your job, protect and serve. LAPD style fool!"

I felt relieved once my stereo installation was completed. Driving home in silence, I tried to think of a polite way to tell my little cousin it was not a good idea for us to hang out anymore. It was hard because I knew Ray felt special hanging out with his cousin the LAPD officer.

Before I could summon up the courage to tell him, Ray spoke first. "You're gonna have to stop coming around so much. You're bad for my reputation. I worked hard for it. You're gonna mess it up."

"Your rep. What about mine?" I shouted.

I was fortunate to have gotten out of that situation alive and without losing my job. As Ray requested, I stopped visiting him so much.

Three weeks later, Ray was arrested for robbery and subsequently sentenced to seven years in a Northern California Prison. Unfortunately, he didn't get a chance to see the birth of his son nor would he be around to raise him as planned.

WHITE AREA

"I was always terribly conscious of this because my dad was a four-star bigot. I used to cringe when he said the "N" word.

Former LAPD chief Daryl Gates referring to his father. ("My life in the LAPD, Chief Daryl F. Gates" July 1992)

West Los Angeles Division in 1989 was not the place for a Black man. Majority of the training officers in West LA Division were twenty-year veterans who were passing time until retirement. A few were brand new training officers with barely two years of valley experience under their belt. My first training officer was a tall, thin Italian man with ten years on the job. He never stopped moving. He was always chewing gum, squirming around in his seat and playing with his hair. At first, I thought he was on crack cocaine but I soon learned that was just the way he was.

The first day, he told me that a police officer's primary objectives were to stay alive, to stay dry, and to stay full. After giving me that important information, we went to a little hamburger stand on Pico Blvd called Big Tommy's Burgers.

"What are you going to order partner?" he asked.

Underneath my nervousness protruded a touch of cockiness. I wanted to impress my training officer more than anything. In a calm and cool voice I replied, "I'll just take whatever you have. I can eat anything."

Since it was only 6:45 a.m., I naturally assumed my partner was going to order breakfast food.

235

How can a person go wrong by ordering breakfast food?

Looking at the cashier, my partner said, "Give me two of the usuals."

Verifying my partner's order, the cashier asked, "Okay, that will be two double chili cheeseburgers, two large orders of chili cheese fries, and two diet Cokes right?"

"Yep, that's it!" Turning toward me he said, "I have been eating here every morning for two years. I eat the same thing every day."

I was accustomed to eating oatmeal and pancakes for breakfast. There was no way I could hold in my first day jitters and eat a chili cheeseburger and fries at 6:45 a.m. but I couldn't punk out after trying so hard to sound tough. After eating the breakfast of champions, my stomach churned and bloated as I fought hard not to take a dump all over myself. Nervousness and chili didn't mix.

Shortly after leaving the hamburger stand, my partner spotted a young, unkempt looking Black man walking down a residential street. My partner immediately stopped the car, got out and handcuffed the young man. He removed the man's identification from his wallet and then ran him for wants and warrants.

"Here is our first arrest partner." He joyously shouted with a smile. "He has a two hundred and fifty dollar misdemeanor warrant for his arrest."

In the academy, I was taught that an officer needed reasonable suspicion to stop and detain someone. I didn't see any just cause to stop the man other than he was a Black man walking in a White neighborhood.

236

Back at the station my partner handed me a computer printout with a bunch of numbers on it and then told me to go book the arrestee. I curiously asked him why we chose to stop the man.

"Well partner, there have been a lot of burglaries on that street lately. According to the reports I have read, most of the burglaries happened between 6:30 a.m. and noon. That guy was dirty, as if he had been prowling around in bushes or something. Based on that, I suspected that he might be a burglar." He then questioned, "Why do you ask? You don't think I stopped him simply because he was Black do you?"

"Of course not. I was just making sure that we were thinking the same way. That's what I thought but I wasn't sure, thanks!" I cowardly answered.

My partner's explanation validated our actions but I still wondered if my partner would have stopped the man if he would have been an unkempt looking White man.

"Remember this, a good police officer can always find a reason to stop anybody anywhere," he followed.

I escorted my arrestee into the booking cage and handed the jailer the paper my partner gave me.

"You must be new!" The jailer said.

"Yes sir. It's my first day."

The jailer handed me another form and said, "Here, you'll need to fill this booking recommendation form out."

Seconds seemed like minutes as I skimmed over the form. I desperately tried to figure out what went where. I had never seen the form before. I thought maybe someone in the academy must have forgotten to teach my class about the form or perhaps I had dozed off during that lecture.

My arrestee sensing my frustration pointed to the form and carefully explained things.

"The warrant number goes in this box and the amount of the warrant goes right here next to it. All that info should be on the other paper that your training officer gave you."

"How do you know so much about this form?" I asked.

"Because bro, I have been arrested for warrants so many times that I could book myself if I had to. You know what I'm sayin?"

"I know what'cha sayin G. Thanks." I replied. "So what wuz you doin over there any way?"

"I wuz minin my own business. That's what I wuz doin when that redneck stopped me. If I would have kept my butt in South Central LA this wouldn't have happened," he said.

"Why not?"

"Cause, a two hundred and fifty dollar warrant ain't nothin! Nobody got time fo dat little ole foolishness in South Central LA."

"If I make it off probation I am going down there," I said.

"You'll make it off probation if you watch out for *doze* rednecks. They want a brotha to fail because we'll find out that they dirty. Your training officer should have made sure that you knew how to fill that form out be-fo you came in here. He didn't because he wanted you to fail Black man! You know what I'm sayin?" The man preached, "If you wuz a White boy, he would have *showed* you how to do it."

My first day showed me I didn't know anything about the job. It also showed me that racial issues were probably the most thought of and feared issues the department faced. Before becoming a police officer, I had worked for two Black operated establishments. Both businesses had all Black clientele and were located in all Black neighborhoods. I only interacted with White people and dealt with racial issues when I wanted. As a police officer, the issue of race tugged at me from both sides.

A lot went through my mind that first day. I wondered if my arrestee was accurate in his assumptions. If he was, what was his motive for telling me? Was he informing me as a Black man who was trying to help his brother? Was he trying to raise my consciousness for my own good? Or was he acting as a selfish criminal by trying to cause friction among his enemies and capturers.

Either way, there was no way I could effectively work as a police officer and question my partner's motives for every arrest. Regardless of my personal feelings, I couldn't openly agree with arrestees in their suspicions of racism. Something had to give. I decided that I would suppress all my doubts and focus on learning the tricks of the trade so I could later do things the right way.

My next training officer was labeled as the toughest and the meanest training officer in the whole entire West Bureau. He was rumored to be a racist, sexist and just down right mean. Everyone including sergeants hated him. He openly bragged about making his female probationers cry.

Before I entered the patrol car, my training officer poked me in the chest with his finger and said, "Look, I'm going to be honest. There are people on this job that don't belong here. They are only here because they are Black, Mexican or because they are female. If you slid through the system, I will find out."

Once in the car, he hit me with a barrage of personal questions like, "Where did you grow up?" "Where do your parents work and where did you go to school." During the course of the conversation, I informed him I was an Assistant Manager and a Loan Officer of a bank before I came on the job. Coincidentally, my training officer and his fiancée were thinking about buying a house. I told him to stop the car. I then got out of the car, opened the trunk and got my calculator out of my bag.

For two hours while parked, I added up all my training officer's bills. I then figured out his debt ratio and approximated his monthly mortgage payments on fixed and variable loans. I gave him the advantages and disadvantages of money market accounts. At the end of the day, my training officer wrote a three-page daily log entry complimenting me on my professionalism and superior job skills. He wrote all that despite only handling three calls.

My old training officer approached me two days later. "I heard your new training officer bragging about you in the locker room. What did you do? Did you shoot somebody or something? He never brags about anyone especially Black people," he said.

Years later, I was not surprised to learn my new training officer was the subject of a sexual harassment investigation. Finally in April, my rookie year in hell was about to come to an end. I couldn't wait to get the hell out of the West LA Division.

As bad as it appeared, West LA wasn't a complete nightmare. I had a few good memories. One night while working with a female training officer, I responded to a screaming woman call at three in the morning in Bel Air. As we pulled up to the location of the call with our lights and siren blaring, I saw a Black man with a long Jheri curl, black tights and boots climbing the fence of a huge immaculate mansion.

My partner yelled, "He doesn't belong up here. Stop him!"

The man looked at us and started running down the street. I jumped out of the car, pointed my gun at the man and ordered him not to move. The man raised his hands and froze in his tracks. Looking into the man's eyes, my breath began to shorten and feel as though I was going to faint. While still pointing my gun at the man, I slightly turned my head toward my partner and whispered, "That's Rick James."

My partner who was strictly a Barry Manilow, Neil Diamond type of gal asked, "Oh, is he a friend of yours?"

"No, that is the famous singer Rick James."

"Sorry, never heard of him," she said.

Still pointing my gun, I began to hum his most popular song "Super Freak" to my training officer. Angrily interrupting me, she said, "I don't care who he is! Make him lay on the ground."

Like a good probationer, I ordered the late singer down to the ground. I put my knee in the singer's back and handcuffed him. In my official police voice, as if I didn't already know, I asked him what his name was.

Nervously stuttering, he answered, "My name is Rick James. I'm a professional singer."

Proning Rick James out was like laying out my own mother. I idolized the man. I even wanted to get my hair braided like Rick's.

"Not while you are living in my house!" my mother said.

Systematically searching him, I ran my hands across the singer's body and searched him for weapons. As I searched him, I couldn't believe I was actually touching Rick James. Back in the day, he was the king of funk music. I would dance for hours at parties to his songs, "Super Freak," "Busting Out," "Mary Jane" and "Dream Maker." His music was very instrumental in the development of my youthful coolness.

After I concluded the search with negative results, I asked him what he was doing climbing fences at three in the morning. Rick began rambling about a new album he was working on.

"Yo man, where have you been? You haven't had an album out in nine years," I said. "What's the problem Rick?"

The more he rambled, the more I realized he was under the influence of something. As it turned out, he was at a party and the host tried to throw him out. He wouldn't leave so she called the police screaming.

Before I released him, I asked my training officer if I could get his autograph.

"Why don't you write him a ticket for being drunk in public and have him autograph that?"

I declined to write my teenage idol a citation. In return I got written up by my training officer for lacking initiative. She said that I let my personal feelings get in the way of doing my job. She also wrote that I jeopardized her life by not remaining focused.

"If that would have been Neil Diamond or Barry Manilow, would you have made one of them lie down on the ground?" I asked her.

"Probably not but he wasn't either of them."

Many officers considered West LA Division to be an excellent place to work because of the affluent citizens and the beautiful surroundings. My traumatic experience while on probation caused me to solemnly swear never to return but I did, nine years later.

EPILOGUE

When I left the prison that day, I left a big part of myself inside the prison with Ray and his comrades. From that day on, my arrestees became more than just a booking number and a statistic. They became a booking number and a statistic with a story behind them.

No matter how much I tried to rationalize my actions or come to grips with my feelings about South Central LA, things still came out the same. People got cursed at! Citizens got beat and people got killed! As a police officer in da hood, there was no way around these things. That was why so many officers left the division.

My first partner, "the good-ole boy" whom I worked with when I first arrived at Southwest Division, resigned from LAPD and is now working as a police officer in the state of Colorado. The country and western music listening, truck driving good-ole boy left LAPD for higher pay and better benefits.

My Black female partner whom I worked with during the 1992 LA riot resigned from the job. She left with a host of personnel complaints and one off-duty related indictment. Allegedly, she took some property that belonged to her neighbor without their permission.

The blonde female officer who refused to go into *The Jungle* and whose name was switched around on the deployment board is suing the Los Angeles Police Department for sexual harassment. Surprisingly, my name was not mentioned in the suit.

244

My other rude, White female partner from Southwest Division quickly promoted from a training officer to a sergeant in less than a year. Officers in the field rest their careers and lives on her decisions. That's scary!

Cheezy is a training officer at the North Hollywood Division. We seldom talk. I heard that he is still insane. He's still the only police officer whom I've felt safe working with.

Gonzales chose to leave the department on his own instead of waiting to be fired. Later, he was arrested for breaking into cars and stealing stereos.

Dirty Terry retired from LAPD. Before he left, he gave me these words of wisdom. "Get the hell out of South Central LA! It was messed up before you were born and it'll be that way after you die! You can't save the world! Leave the LAPD before it destroys you."

Ironically, the Black female training officer who I had a run in while at West LA Division went off on stress leave. Her claim was the Department racially discriminated against her after the Black captain left the division.

On the same note, the Captain of West LA Division is now a commander and one of the highest-ranking officers on the department. There is a good chance he may one day become the Chief of police for LAPD.

On a personal note, my cousin Ray received an early release from prison for good behavior. When he came home, he spent each and every day with his son. He walked him to nursery school and read him bedtime stories every night before going to bed. He was the perfect father. A month and a half later, Ray was arrested for burglary and given a three strikes sentence of forty-five years to life in prison.

What about me? I'm still working at the Southwest Division. I'm still catching criminals and picking up personnel complaints. In fact, one time...

END

BIBLIOGRAPHY

Former LAPD chief Daryl Gates, My life in the LAPD, Chief Daryl F. Gates, Bantam Books, July 1992.

Former LAPD detective Mark Fuhrman, transcripts used by the O.J Simpson defense lawyers.

Sanyika Shakur, A.K.A. Monster Kody Scott, Monster, the Autobiography of an L.A. Gang Member, The Atlantic Monthly Press, (1993)

Made in United States
North Haven, CT
02 August 2024

55684339R00139